Seek for the CITY 2013

When times are tough our prayers can tend to focus on our fears and our needs. Crisis prayers often dwindle to cries for no more than our own survival. Why not pray instead for God to fulfill His greatest promises? What better time will there ever be for God to be glorified as He acts in response to the united prayer of His people?

This prayer guide is designed to help everyday believers pray beyond their daily needs and further than their fears. Leaders of a previous generation would have called them "extraordinary prayers" because they call on God to fulfill His greatest purposes.

Like few other times in history, now is an hour to pray in confident expectancy of what Christ will accomplish. May Christ increase our love and strengthen our faith as we unite in prayers of hope.

Yours in hope of Christ's glory,

Steve Hawthorne for WayMakers

Helping others join with you
Praying *with* others

We always pray better together. Well over 150,000 believers from many hundreds of churches will be praying these prayers. So you won't be praying alone.

Find and share practical ideas. Use the helpful resources at **waymakers.org**. Find practical ways to remind your church family to pray such as bulletin inserts and powerpoint slides. Interact with others about what you like about the prayers at **Facebook.com/seekgodforthecity**.

The Spanish translation.
Invite Spanish-speaking friends to pray with *Seek God For The City 2013* in Spanish. It's called *Clama a Dios por la Ciudad 2013*. The 64-page booklet is available at the same low cost as the English version. Available December, 2012. Order at **waymakers.org**.

Pray with the kids. A children's companion version. 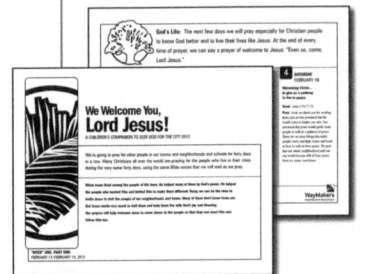
A free, downloadable kid's version is available in "pdf" format on our website. It's a great resource to engage kids in this prayer adventure! Find it at **waymakers.org**.

Now it's an app. To pray as you go. 
You can also get *Seek God for the City* as an app for your smartphone or tablet (Apple or Android). The app contains all of the same scriptures, prayers and helpful material. Available December, 2012. Check out a preview at **waymakers.org**. The app makes it possible for many more people to use *Seek God* where it may be difficult to carry or transport copies of the booklet. Start telling your friends in other cities and countries now.

iOS   Android

Helping you pray for others
Praying *for* others

Prayer leads to **Care** and opens ways to **Share**.

This prayer guide is not intended as a guide for your personal devotions. It's designed to help you extend your life, your love and your prayers for others. Praying in hope becomes a way of joining God in His great love.

Persistent, life-giving **prayer** for others...

God is calling us to pray beyond the boundaries of our homes and lives. He's giving us ways to advance His work in the lives of neighbors and co-workers by praying for them. As you learn to pray with biblical hope, you will find yourself praying your way into the story of what God is already unfolding in their lives.

...leads to opportunities to **care**, displaying God's love...

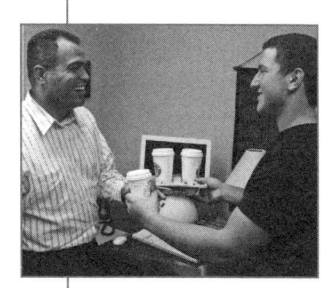

Praying for others will help you keep alert to the ways that you might be able to demonstrate God's love in practical, tangible ways. As you walk through doors that God opens to display His love, you'll discover a growing sense of adventure, compassion and mission with God.

...that opens the way to **share** the gospel, declaring God's love.

As you continue to pray and to show God's love in practical ways, you'll find that God often gives you creative ways to communicate with people about how they can follow Jesus. Instead of dreading evangelism as if it were a burden, you'll find yourself following God's lead with timely authenticity and sincerity.

*For more about growing in a prayer-care-share lifestyle, go to **www.waymakers.org**. You'll find practical ideas and links to resources and stories of other leaders.*

"Fulfill-it Prayers" in a Small Town
by John McGarvey

As a church we had used *Seek God for the City* a few times in the past. I've always appreciated that the focus is on hope-based prayers, not simply need-based prayers, or as we like to put it, instead of "fix-it" prayers, we are praying "fulfill-it" prayers.

Churches praying together. The booklet was so well received by our congregation in 2011 that I showed it to other pastors in our local ministerial association. In 2012 several churches in the community participated together. It began with the simple idea that we would all be going through the material at the same time.

Praying like Daniel. During the 40 days of *Seek God*, I preached a series of messages from the book of Daniel. Even as a small town we deal with the impact of sin. At one point we looked at the prayer in Daniel 9 and we noted the desolation of sin and Daniel's sense of urgency. We realized that there are times when God's people decide that things cannot go on as they are. We began to pray from Daniel 9 in the same kind of "fulfill-it" way that we had been praying in *Seek God for the City*:

John McGarvey with others about to prayerwalk different parts of Cochranton on the first Saturday of the month, a practice which began after using Seek God for the City.

> God, we have had enough of desolation! We pray that our neighborhoods would be a place where instead of desolation, Your promises are fulfilled, Your mighty acts made known, Your character revealed, Your glory displayed. Expose the darkness and shine the Light! Bring forgiveness and hope. Living God, begin right now to make a name for Yourself in our neighborhood!

Steps toward a town revitalized. Some months before our "Daniel" praying along with *Seek God*, some local business and community leaders formed a group (Cochranton Area Redevelopment Effort, or "CARE") to work on a broad-based revitalization of the community. Seeing that there was a need for a spiritual revitalization as well, our ministerial association had already pledged the support of the churches. The united prayer effort opened our eyes and our hopes to what spiritual revitalization might look like.

Ongoing expectation and hope. As *Seek God for the City 2012* got underway, God began to work in a variety of ways. One of the outcomes was that some believers from different churches have been coming together on the first Saturday of every month to pray for our community. There has been a sense of expectation as we seek the Lord together. Our only agenda is the fulfillment of God's purposes.

John McGarvey pastors the Christian and Missionary Alliance Church in Cochranton, Pennsylvania, a small community of about 1200 people.

Many Churches Praying Together
by Andrea Sanger

Pastors in the Coachella Valley began to dream about finding a way to get a large number of people to be praying the same thing on the same day, and then watch for what God might do. After a little research, they decided that *Seek God for the City* would be the right tool to help churches to pray together.

Easy to organize combined orders. First, we got review copies of *Seek God for the City*–in both English and Spanish–into the hands of all the pastors. Two key churches started things off by sponsoring orders of 500 copies each. We continued to pool orders from the various churches to get the low per-thousand price for every church. At our monthly luncheon for pastors, we collected orders, and discussed how we would use the prayer guides. Combining orders for English and Spanish copies allowed us to get the lowest price for churches of any size. Turnaround on our orders was quick, making it easy to distribute the booklets at the next luncheon.

Pastors discuss plans over lunch to use Seek God for the City as a way of helping their people grow in a "Prayer-Care-Share" lifestyle. Orders were pooled at the meeting to reduce cost.

Bridging the gaps of age and language. The report back from the different churches, ministries and Christian schools in our area was phenomenal. The booklet made it possible to breach the gaps in prayer, both cross-culturally and cross-generationally:

- *Both English and Spanish speaking churches* reported that the booklets helped their weekly prayer times.
- *Christian schools.* A Christian elementary school was using the children's companion version during their "flag time" each morning. The kids were loving it. A Christian high school was using it as their morning devotional. Students began to look forward to it every day.
- *A choir prepared.* One church choir prayed through it together. Choir practice fell on the very day that *Seek God for the City* called for prayer for the homeless. As they left the rehearsal they encountered a homeless person. They were ready to minister to this man because they had their hearts prepared to help him.

To get everyone involved took a bit of time and organization, but it was well worth the effort. We will be doing it again in the future.

Andrea Sanger is part of the LOV Movement (Lighthouses Of the Valley) in the Coachella Valley (greater Palm Springs, California). The LOV Movement integrates a "Prayer, Care and Share" strategy to present the love of Christ where people live and work throughout the Coachella Valley.

Our Family Loved the App
by Casey and Mandi Morgan

We're always looking for ways to expose and engage our family with meaningful connections with God's plan to bring and redeem worship from all nations. Since three of our kids have been adopted from other countries, many of the themes of *Seek God for the City* really resonate with us.

The app was easy for our family. We've decided not to have a television at home. So our kids' consumption of media is through portable devices—iPads, smart phones and the web. We've used *Seek God* before, but the mobile app format made it a natural for our kids. The app made it seamless and easy for them to use. They were the ones clicking on the different prayers and on the specific affinity groups. The app was so well-designed that our kids took turns navigating through it, leading different parts of our prayer time.

How we did it as a family. Our family has about a 10 to 15 minute time together in the morning before we all head out the door. We found that *Seek God for the City* worked perfectly in this quick time slot. We took turns reading the scriptures and the prayers. It's one thing when mom or dad reads a devotional and then we all walk out the door. It's another thing for our nine-year-old to read the scripture out loud, and then our seven-year-old to read the suggested prayer. It's not just a devotional; instead, it's saying, "Hey. Here's who we can pray for, and how we can get started praying for them."

Casey and Mandi adopted three of their six children. The app format made praying through Seek God for the City to be practical for their family. The kids took turns navigating and reading the different parts.

Doable but flexible. I think that if each day had pages and pages of info, it wouldn't have worked for us. But it's set up nice and clean, making it easy to get familiar with the places and parts we wanted to go to. A couple evenings a week we would find one of the prayerwalking ideas (every day has a different one) to do in our neighborhood. It was cool to tap on the buttons for some of the countries that took us to the expanded info on the *Operation World* website. It was fun to watch our ten-year-old say, "I've never heard of Bahrain. Let's go there." He'd click on it and boom! There's Bahrain on a map with some images, and then we're praying as a family. Very cool. We'll definitely be using the *Seek God* app as a family in 2013.

> Check out the app!
> Go to WayMakers.org.
> Available on both Apple and Android platforms.
>
> iOS   Android

*Casey and Mandi Morgan worked for several years in Latin America and East Asia. They and their six kids now live in Arkansas, serving with the ministry Seven Nine. See **www.79online.org**.*

Engaging Our Entire Church
by Milfred Minatrea

My own family's past experience praying through *Seek God for the City* led me to recognize the impact it could have on our congregation. I had just been called as senior pastor of Grand View Baptist Church. Praying through *Seek God* was one of the first church-wide emphases I encouraged our church to embrace.

How we got copies in their hands. Four weeks before starting *Seek God for the City*, we used posters and bulletin inserts to let the entire church family know that copies of the prayer guide would be available on February 12, 15, and 19 for a suggested donation. Volunteers staffed a distribution table before, between and after services.

A sermon series at the same time. During the six Sundays of the 40-day season, I designed a series of sermons called "Seek God for the City." Each of the messages was based on one of the biblical selections found in that week's pages of *Seek God for the City*. The messages invited God to speak directly to our congregation concerning what He desired to accomplish in our city and throughout the world. Each Sunday's worship folder used a graphic design that emulated the *Seek God for the City* booklets.

As gifts to guests. Complimentary copies of *Seek God* were given to all visiting guests during the 40 days. We found guests eager to get a copy, even on the final Sunday of the season. We also delivered a gift copy to the homes of guests who had worshiped with us in the weeks before the 40 days began.

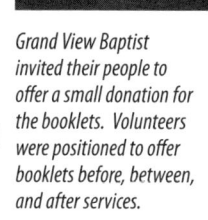

Grand View Baptist invited their people to offer a small donation for the booklets. Volunteers were positioned to offer booklets before, between, and after services.

Stretching our imagination. Readings from *Seek God* informed our weekly prayer gathering. We shared prayer points that had captured our imaginations during the preceding days. We prayed around the world together, for the countries on each page.

Concluding with a crescendo on Palm Sunday. On the 40th day, the mayor of our city worshiped with us and shared the importance of the faith community. He emphasized that when the church is active in ministering and praying for the city, its presence and participation flavor the city with grace and goodness.

Milfred Minatrea is senior pastor of Grand View Baptist Church and also serves as the Director of the Missional Church Center (www.missional.org) in Mesquite, Texas.

A Way to Walk Together
Learning to Practice Prayerwalking
by Peter Koch

I thought *Seek God for the City* would be a good way to have something that I could go through daily and also use to build deeper relationships with some of my friends in my church. So I asked a couple of guys to start praying with me every day in the morning.

Every day a different prayerwalking idea. As we started going through the 40 days, we soon found that every day the prayer guide says to prayerwalk for a particular group. Well, since it says prayerwalk, we figured let's do what it says, and go pray and walk. Each day in *Seek God for the City* has some idea of where to go, like a school, or a business, or a hospital or something. We would try to go somewhere within walking distance if we could do it in a reasonable amount of time. We had classes and jobs, so we would have to get right to it. We would meet at either six or eight every morning.

Peter Koch (center) prayerwalking with two friends near a high school in Los Angeles.

Great way to start the day.
It's such an amazing way to start your day focusing first on God, and then just getting outside to walk and pray. You see things that trigger thoughts in your head of how to pray. What really helped keep us going was that after a couple of weeks, we invited a couple more people to pray with us. We all knew that the other guys were counting on us. We soon had five or six guys every morning.

Why stop? We kept walking on. The prayerwalking helped our walk with Christ in really obvious ways. As the 40 days wound down we couldn't think of any reason to stop, so we decided to just keep going. We kept meeting five days a week for a few months. We've taken a pause for awhile, but we'll probably get going again at least by the next time *Seek God for the City* gets going. Meanwhile, we've started to organize bimonthly prayerwalks with several of the small groups of my church in Pasadena.

Peter Koch is a university student in Pasadena, California. Peter and a few friends used the prayerwalking ideas found on each page of Seek God for the City.

Prayer On the Air
Connecting the Community with Radio
by Wende Davis

Imagine having the chance to unite thousands of people in prayer. This is what *Seek God for the City* did for our radio station, **88.7 The Bridge**. A friend of the station brought *Seek God* to our attention. We decided that it could help fulfill our vision, which is to connect and strengthen our community. Prior to beginning the 40-day event, we heavily promoted *Seek God for the City*, and informed our audience about how they could obtain booklets directly from WayMakers. The response from individuals and churches was truly amazing. By the time Day One came, our community was very excited to start this adventure.

Seek God prayers on-air a few times each day. In order to facilitate a unified community-wide prayer effort, we divided the daily prayer program into four sections: the Old Testament prayer, the New Testament prayer, the subgroup and that day's select nations. Each part was reinforced three times daily on-air. Each week we picked one of the subgroups from that week's prayer topics in *Seek God* as a special focus. We interviewed a different local ministry each week to highlight that focus. We supported the program with a web page and by sending daily texts containing a few words about each day's topic.

Bring them together by broadcasting in your area.
Radio is a powerful media with an influential voice. Like the Bridge, many Christian radio stations desire to reflect the heart of God for the community in their broadcasts. It may be that a station would consider incorporating a season of focused, united prayer as a part of their programming in your community. The hard work has already been done. You only need to implement the provided prayer framework of *Seek God* in a way that is effective and meaningful for your listening audience. Be creative, there are plenty of ways to adapt it. We heard reports of Christ reaching individuals, families and churches with His love and healing touch. We heard many stories about the sense of community people experienced just knowing others were praying in agreement. It will be part of our programming for next year! Please join us as we *Seek God* together!

---

*Wende Davis serves as the prayer coordinator for the Christian radio station **88.7 The Bridge**, broadcasting from Delaware, to a region including much of Maryland, New Jersey and beyond. Find out more at **887thebridge.com**.*

Praying in the Same Direction
Engaging in Scripture to Unite Prayer in New York City
by Gary Frost

In late 2010, pastors and leaders of many churches throughout the city of New York initiated a catalytic plan to mobilize their people to move beyond their secondary differences in order to pursue God's primary purpose of demonstrating the love of Christ to their city. The plan was simple: For 40 days, read and engage with the same scriptures together and then pray from those scriptures for God's purpose. The program was called "NOW Is The Time" and consisted of a simple guide for reading and praying from the book of Nehemiah. The idea was successfully tested in 2011, leading to an even greater participation in the spring of 2012. Over 150 churches called their people to read and pray from the same passages in Nehemiah during the 40 days leading to Pentecost.

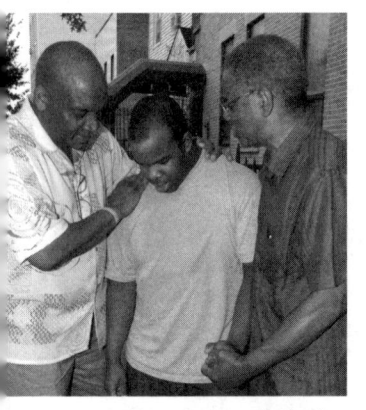

Reading and praying Nehemiah.
The project was a collaborative endeavor between many ministries and churches, among them Concerts of Prayer Greater New York, the American Bible Society, NYC Intercessors and the NYC Leadership Center. While these leaders were preparing a second season of scripture and prayer based on the book of Nehemiah to take place in 2012, we had no idea how relevant and strategic the ancient message of Nehemiah would prove to be.

A ruling against God's people in public.
After a prolonged battle with the City of New York, the New York State Supreme Court determined that religious groups would no longer be allowed to rent public school buildings for worship services. The mayor of New York acted quickly to decree that all churches and religious entities that had been renting school facilities for worship services would be forced to discontinue, almost immediately. The scarcity and cost of facilities in the city meant that many churches would be functionally disbanded.

Above: *Gary Frost (left) and Boswell Bent (right) pray with a neighbor in Brooklyn during one of the many prayerwalks that have been organized by Christians in New York City.*
Opposite page: *Christians from many churches prayed openly about the issue of Christian worship in public school facilities.*

Recognizing the spiritual warfare dimension of this struggle, churches of various denominations, ethnicities and capacities throughout the region came together in prayer. Momentum surged for prayer concerning God's greater purposes in dramatic and public ways. In the spring of 2012, there was a 60% increase of churches from various networks participating in the "NOW Is The Time" program to read and pray from the book of Nehemiah. Nehemiah's project to rebuild the damaged walls and the devastated people of the city of Jerusalem served as a "prayer curriculum," providing guidance and encouragement as we sought divine intervention in the face of intense opposition. Prayer was fervent through the 40 days. It was obvious that only supernatural help could turn back forces of secularism arrayed so clearly against God's people.

An overruling. And a continuing appeal.
And then, God showed up. After months of prayer and fasting, with marches, letters and visits to legislators, and one month after completing the 40 days of prayer, another judge in a higher court issued a permanent injunction in favor of churches having access to schools for worship services, thus overruling the mayor of New York City. There are court battles still ahead. There are great purposes of God in our city that are still unfulfilled. We're going to continue to pray.

Beginning on Pentecost, 2013: Praying Acts in 28 days.
We are inviting Christ's followers in New York (and beyond!) to join us in reading and praying through the book of Acts. This time we'll pray for 28 days (28 chapters) beginning on Pentecost Sunday, May 19, 2013. Once again we'll work in collaboration with the American Bible Society and other partners to engage in daily scripture reading and prayer. If you would like to join us and include your church or city in this initiative, please go to **www.PrayingActs.com** for more information.

*Gary Frost serves as President of Concerts of Prayer Greater New York, a Christ-centered network of pastors and churches promoting a culture of prayer across ethnic, economic and denominational lines. Learn more at **www.copgny.org**.*

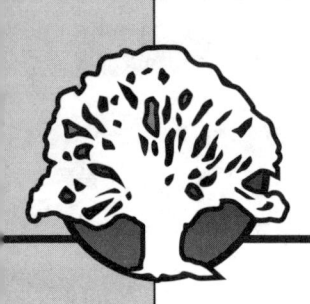

Seeking His **Life**
to Revive the Church

FEBRUARY 13-23　WEEK 1

This "week" (actually an 11 day period, beginning on Ash Wednesday, February 13) we will pray toward the hope of God reviving His people with spiritual life.

As you pray for God's people in your city, you will be praying along with many thousands of others who will be asking God to bring life to the churches throughout their own communities. Of course, pray for your own church. But be sure to pray for the life and unity of many churches, so that together, God's people would freshly experience the splendor of His power and life so that we will become Christ's instruments to complete His purposes throughout the earth.

The Americas and the Caribbean

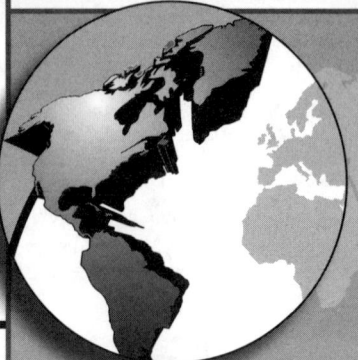

During the 40 days, we'll be praying for the continental areas of the earth in reverse sequence of Acts 1:8. Thus, we begin at one of the areas of the earth farthest from Jerusalem. We'll start by praying for the continents of South and North America and the Caribbean.

SEEK GOD
...for His forgiveness and joy to bring revival

Day 1
WEDNESDAY
FEBRUARY 13

You forgave the iniquity of Your people; You covered all their sin. Selah... Restore us, O God of our salvation... Will You not Yourself revive us again, that Your people may rejoice in You?
— Psalm 85:2, 4, 6

You have loved each one of us as a son or as a daughter. But we also stand before You as a people—Your people. And as Your people, we are ashamed to confess that we continue to return over and over to the very sins You have already washed away. We humbly seek Your forgiveness once again. But yet we seek more than just another round of forgiveness. We want more than a clean slate. Do not merely restore us, but transform us by Your powerful love. Sustain us with increasing love for You so that we may stand before You as a people in confident joy.

His father saw him and felt compassion... the son said to him, "Father, I have sinned against heaven and in your sight."...But the father said to his slaves, "Quickly bring out the best robe... let us eat and celebrate; for this son of mine was dead and has come to life again."...And they began to celebrate.
— Luke 15:20-24

Why are we surprised that Your heart overflows in party-starting joy whenever a long lost son or daughter comes home? Whenever we turn towards You, even slightly, we find that You have already been seeking us. What vigilant love! What extravagant gladness! To come home to You, and sense Your delight, is like coming back to life from the dead. Make us jubilant in Your house so that many more in our city will find their way home to You. *Pray:*

- For God's love and joy to be revealed, resulting in many coming alive to God.
- For many people to experience the reviving mercy of God.

Seek God on behalf of **Youth**

For teens to radically and completely commit their lives to Christ; to make wise choices; for older mentors; for authentic friendships with their peers who are following Jesus; for open trust and communication with parents; for God's intentions for their generation to come forth in fullest measure.

Prayerwalk: Pray with your eyes open for people in their teens. Envision them following Christ five, ten or more years from now.

Let our sons in their youth be as grown-up plants, and our daughters as corner pillars fashioned as for a palace...How blessed are the people whose God is the LORD!
— Psalm 144:12, 15

Seek God on behalf of **the Americas and the Caribbean**
Anguilla, Antigua and Barbuda, Argentina, Aruba, Bahamas

Day 2

**THURSDAY
FEBRUARY 14**

SEEK GOD
...for the revelation of God's love

*Show us Your lovingkindness, O LORD, and grant us Your salvation.
I will hear what God the LORD will say; for He will speak peace to His people, to His godly ones; but let them not turn back to folly.* – Psalm 85:7-8

Free us from the folly of seeking to be inspired rather than to be changed. We agree with the sermons about salvation. We are thrilled with reports about Your reviving power. But we have failed to change our ways. We find ourselves turning back to stubborn habits of heart again and again. We have proved the folly of merely deciding to be different. Only You can change us. Reveal the magnificent love of Christ as never before. We will listen for Your voice, speaking Your life-changing word in a way that brings about a deep and lasting difference. Declare Your peace with such power so that we are transfigured to live in the fullness of Christ's life.

He who has My commandments and keeps them is the one who loves Me; and he who loves Me will be loved by My Father, and I will love him and will disclose Myself to him. – John 14:21

Lord Jesus, You know our hearts. You see our sincere but erratic efforts to serve You. Because of Your vast, forever love, even our feeble attempts to obey You end up delighting You. We have perceived only the tiniest bit of Your great love. As You promised, show us more and more of Yourself. The more we experience Your love, the more we will find ourselves obeying You with joy. *Pray:*

- For God's love to be revealed afresh to hardened backsliders.
- For Christ to encounter struggling believers with heart-changing clarity, so that they live in Christ's power.

Seek God on behalf of **Families**

For solid, God-centered relationships among family members; that parents would be bold to instruct their children in God's way of living and lead their families to pray together; for families dismantled by divorce to be healed; that Christ's forgiveness would dissolve long-held anger.

In you and in your descendants shall all the families of the earth be blessed.
– Genesis 28:14

Prayerwalk: Prayerwalk as a family through your own neighborhood. Ask God to give you family-to-family prayers of blessing for two or three families.

Seek God on behalf of **the Americas and the Caribbean**

Barbados, Belize, Bermuda, Bolivia, Brazil

SEEK GOD
...for revival bringing salvation and glory

Day 3
FRIDAY
FEBRUARY 15

Surely His salvation is near to those who fear Him, that glory may dwell in our land. – Psalm 85:9

We are familiar with the truth that Jesus is our Savior. Bring us into an encounter with Jesus as the Living One, risen from the dead, presiding now in our midst. Allow our hearts to fill with awe concerning Your great purpose. You have saved us for more than merely having a better life and a brighter afterlife. You have saved us so that we might walk, breathe and speak like You–that Your glory would be seen in our lives and in our land. Postponing the hope of Your glory until the age to come has dishonored You. We pray now for You to fulfill Your purpose in us. Continually save us and fill us in these days, so that we reflect Your love and glory.

Martha said to Him, "I know that he will rise again in the resurrection on the last day." Jesus said to her, "I am the resurrection and the life...Did I not say to you that if you believe, you will see the glory of God?" – John 11:24-25, 40

Risen Jesus, we must answer "Yes" to Your question. Yes, we believe that we will see the glory of God in our day. We choose to set aside our despair. You were raised to overcome our broken hopes. We believe in You as the Risen One. Bring Your life to many, and with Your life, show Your brilliant glory. *Pray:*

- For believers to be filled with renewed expectation that God's glory will be revealed in our day.
- For the despairing to experience new hope that they will see the goodness of God in the land of the living.
- That friends and family would trust in Jesus Christ, and by faith, behold His glory.

Seek God on behalf of **Women**

That women will be honored in their unique, God-created glory; that every kind of injustice toward women will cease; for pornography to be stopped; for protection from sexual violence; that hope would be renewed for the beauty of marriage and children; that single women would lay hold of God's full purpose in their lives.

This woman was abounding with deeds of kindness and charity which she continually did.
– Acts 9:36

Prayerwalk: Without being demonstrative, pray prayers of blessing for some of the women you come in contact with today.

Seek God on behalf of **the Americas and the Caribbean**
British Virgin Islands, Canada, Cayman Islands, Chile, Colombia

Day 4

SATURDAY
FEBRUARY 16

SEEK GOD
...for revival bringing righteousness and peace

Righteousness and peace have kissed each other. Truth springs from the earth, and righteousness looks down from heaven. Indeed, the LORD will give what is good, and our land will yield its produce. Righteousness will go before Him and will make His footsteps into a way. – Psalm 85:10-13

Our hearts yearn for the life of God to be planted and to thrive in our city. We are like a wild, untended garden that has been fruitless before You. Sow the seed of the truth in many lives. Come like the sun with Your power. Come like the rain with Your Spirit. Cultivate our community patiently and bring forth lives marked by Christ's righteousness. Cause Your presence to come upon us, as if You were walking step by step ahead of us, marking out Your way of living abundantly.

For you will...prepare His ways; to give to His people the knowledge of salvation by the forgiveness of their sins...to guide our feet into the way of peace.
– Luke 1: 76-77, 79

It was promised, Lord Jesus, that when You came, many would experience forgiveness of sins. And so it came to pass; and so it continues today. But Your salvation came with a further promise, that we would learn how to live in the magnificent power and joy of heaven's peace. Visit us in peace-bringing power. Guide us step by step to live in Your ways of peace, and gradually bring lasting transformation to our entire community.
Pray:

- For Christian friends to experience as never before Christ's guiding presence.
- For believers to walk in the righteousness of God, influencing the economy, values and character of their entire community.

Seek God on behalf of **Single People**

Pray that Christ will fill singles' hearts with His love; that they may taste the satisfaction which is found only in God; that friendships will bring ample fullness of relationship; for sexual purity and simplicity of lifestyle; and strong marriages for those who desire them. Pray for those single by divorce or death, that they would find healing and new hope for life ahead.

Prayerwalk: Bless those people who are single. Consider their story. Pray for their future and hopes.

One who is unmarried is concerned about the things of the Lord, how he may please the Lord.
– 1 Corinthians 7:32

Seek God on behalf of **the Americas and the Caribbean**
Costa Rica, Cuba, Dominica, Dominican Republic, Ecuador

SEEK GOD
...to restore His people to fruitfulness

Day 5
SUNDAY
FEBRUARY 17

Turn again, O God of hosts; look down from heaven, and see; have regard for this vine, the stock that Your right hand planted...But let Your hand be upon the one...whom You made strong for Yourself. Then we will never turn back from You. Give us life, and we will call on Your name.
– Psalm 80:14-15, 17-18 (NRSV)

We are like a hand-planted garden in Your sight. You intend for us to bloom with Your beauty and multiply Your life in others. Like a vineyard keeper watches his vineyard, You constantly examine us. You see that we are alive, but often fruitless. We have produced leaves but little more. Do not merely look on us from afar. Come near to us. Extend Your hand, the very hand that formed us, in order to restore us. Stretch us and strengthen us to grow in Your glory, presenting to You the lasting fruit of families and friends who praise Your name.

I am the true vine, and My Father is the vinedresser. Every branch in Me that does not bear fruit, He takes away [literally: He lifts]...I am the vine, you are the branches; he who abides in Me and I in him, he bears much fruit.
– John 15:1-2, 5

You have destined us to bear much fruit. But You have often found us barren. May the Father lift us from the mud where He has found us, some of us shriveled and fruitless. Stretch us upward, staking us and holding us open before the light of heaven. May the power of Christ's life course through us to bring forth what pleases You. *Pray:*

- For believers to be stretched in spiritual disciplines so that they impart spiritual life to others.
- For despondent believers to be lifted into the light of God's presence.
- For God to renew churches so that they increase in Christ's character.

Seek God on behalf of **International Visitors**

For students, workers and businesspeople from other lands to be treated with honor and respect; that they will enjoy new friendships; that they will encounter the message of the gospel clearly declared and lovingly demonstrated.

Prayerwalk: Find a public place or business which draws international visitors or students. As you see people from different nations, pray God's blessing on them and their home countries.

Assemble the people—men, women and children, and the aliens living in your towns—so they can listen and learn to fear the LORD your God.
– Deuteronomy 31:12 (NIV)

Seek God on behalf of **the Americas and the Caribbean**
El Salvador, Falkland Islands, French Guiana, Greenland

Day 6

MONDAY
FEBRUARY 18

SEEK GOD
...to impart His life-giving Spirit

*"Son of man, can these bones live?"
I answered, "O Lord GOD, You know."
..."Behold, I will cause breath to enter
you that you may come to life."
...So I prophesied as He commanded me,
and the breath came into them, and they
came to life and stood on their feet.
..."I will put My Spirit within you
and you will come to life."*
— Ezekiel 37:3, 5, 10, 14

We pray on behalf of those who are physically alive but are spiritually dead. Breathe life into them, as You did at creation. Infuse them with Your Spirit. As Ezekiel did so long ago, we declare our prayer: "Come to life! He will put His Spirit within you and you will come to life!" Come upon us, Spirit of God! Resuscitate those who have suffocated in their sin. Renew those who have wavered in their love for You. Surprise many who have not yet known You. Raise up great throngs of people throughout the earth to stand before You, filled with life and eager to serve.

*Truly, truly, I say to you, an hour is
coming and now is, when the dead
will hear the voice of the Son of God,
and those who hear will live.* — John 5:25

From the day You rose from the grave, those who are dead in spirit have been coming to life by the power of Your word. It's time in our town for many to hear Your voice and live. Only Your voice gives life. A whisper from You can wake our friends. One word can wake our churches. A shout can raise people throughout our city. Lift Your voice, Son of God! Raise many to fullness of life. *Pray:*

- For dead or dying churches in your city to be renewed in Christ's life.
- For the word of God to be heard and for His life-giving Spirit to be received by many who are far from God.
- For a special season when many will pay attention, with clear hearing, to the word of God.

Seek God on behalf of **Gangs**

That God will satisfy their deep desires for significance and belonging; for God to break the spiritual and social powers that hold them; for caring Christians to embrace them in the authentic love of God's family; for blessing upon the neighborhoods they claim.

Prayerwalk: Pray at a place affected by gang activity. Speak God's Word as you walk to spiritually "tag" the territories with unseen but real declarations of His Lordship, love and blessing.

*Help, LORD, for the godly
man ceases to be, for the
faithful disappear from
among the sons of men....
"Now I will arise," says the
LORD, "I will set him in the
safety for which he longs."*
— Psalm 12:1, 5

Seek God on behalf of **the Americas and the Caribbean**
Grenada, Guadeloupe, Guatemala, Guyana, Haiti

SEEK GOD
...for Christ's resurrection power

Day 7
TUESDAY
FEBRUARY 19

Come, let us return to the LORD. For He has torn us, but He will heal us; He has wounded us, but He will bandage us. He will revive us after two days; He will raise us up on the third day, that we may live before Him.
— Hosea 6:1-2

We have grieved You greatly by our sin. But we have harmed ourselves far more. You have allowed the consequences of our sin to fall upon us. Wounded, we ran from You, blaming You for our pain. Even so, You have preserved us for a time of turning to You. May this be the time of turning and a day of healing for many of our city. May we be the first of many more that will return to You. The healing of our broken souls may not happen instantly. Help us to wait patiently for Your healing to renew us fully. Days or weeks may pass, but surely You will revive those You have loved to live before You.

When I saw Him, I fell at His feet like a dead man. And He placed His right hand on me, saying, "Do not be afraid; I am the first and the last, and the living One; and I was dead, and behold, I am alive forevermore, and I have the keys of death and of Hades."
— Revelation 1:17-18

Lord Jesus, You are the Living One, alive with a different kind of life. A mere glimpse of Your majesty caused Your closest friend to fall at Your feet as if he were dead. Then You touched him; and spoke to him, forbidding him to fear. Touch us, too, Living One. Speak to our hearts and lift us from our fears. Empower us with Your life. Unlock the doors of death that hold many of our city in darkness. *Pray:*

- For Christians to encounter the risen Jesus in the beauty of His glory.
- For the authority of Christ to liberate people from the grip of sin, the fear of death and the deception of evil powers.

Seek God on behalf of **Marriages**

Thank God for sturdy marriages that reflect His faithfulness and beauty. Pray especially for marriages which are strained to a breaking point or are failing, that God will bring both hope and help; that He will heal broken hearts and restore intimacy; for every marriage, that God will refresh and re-center homes in Christ.

Marriage should be honored by all.
— Hebrews 13:4 (NIV)

Prayerwalk: Pray with your spouse (if married) near the homes that may need a special touch of God's healing upon marriages.

Seek God on behalf of **the Americas and the Caribbean**
Honduras, Jamaica, Martinique, Mexico, Montserrat

Day 8

WEDNESDAY
FEBRUARY 20

SEEK GOD
...to purify His people

Purify me with hyssop, and I shall be clean. Wash me, and I shall be whiter than snow...Create in me a clean heart, O God, and renew a steadfast spirit within me. — Psalm 51:7, 10

We've tried to find ways to purge ourselves from feelings of guilt and shame. But self-help therapy or religious fervency often darken the stains. Instead, we renounce every preposterous thought that we could ever make ourselves pure. Wash us clean. Free us from the lingering power of sin. Wash away the sense of disgrace and distance from You. Give us confidence that we are clean and pleasing before You. Remake many hearts at once throughout our city. Renew us as a people from the inside so that we are steady and strong to serve You in this hour.

Blessed are the pure in heart, for they shall see God. — Matthew 5:8

We have no hope of being pure on our own. Unless You purify our hearts we can't even turn our eyes toward You. Do Your work, Lord Jesus. Simplify the motives of our hearts. Clear the clutter of competing desires. Give us a simple, single-hearted passion for You. Align our scattered thoughts and focus our hopes so that the only thing that matters is that You will be seen and loved by all. *Pray:*

- For non-believers to see the difference between superficial religious behavior and genuine heart purity before God.
- For believers to confess and abandon patterns of sin.
- For many to be moved to seek God wholeheartedly.

Seek God on behalf of **Sick People**

That God will touch those who are sick in your community with healing and comfort; that they will grow in grace as God walks with them throughout their ordeal; that God will provide for their financial needs; for their caregivers and families; that many will renew their trust in Christ and follow Him boldly, even in affliction.

He saw a large crowd, and felt compassion for them and healed their sick. — Matthew 14:14

Prayerwalk: Consider those who may be struggling with chronic illness or pain in your neighborhood. Pray for their healing.

Seek God on behalf of **the Americas and the Caribbean**

Netherlands Antilles, Nicaragua, Panama, Paraguay, Peru

SEEK GOD
...for His people to love and obey Him

Day 9
THURSDAY
FEBRUARY 21

*I have set before you life and death...
So choose life in order that you may live
...by loving the LORD your God, by
obeying His voice, and by holding fast
to Him; for this is your life and the
length of your days.*
— Deuteronomy 30:19-20

How easy it would be for You to force our obedience. At any moment You could commandeer our minds and program our souls to obey with never-failing precision. But You desire genuine love rather than robotic religious behavior. Real love responds to Your voice with daily, diligent choices to prefer and serve You. We have said "Yes" to You before. And yet we still wander away, enticed to small compromises and foolish distractions. Please keep speaking to us. Let us hear Your voice, and we'll obey You. Let us sense the touch of Your hand, and we'll cling to You. Steady our wobbly affections so that our love for You will increase throughout our days.

*No servant can serve two masters;
for either he will hate the one and love
the other, or else he will be devoted
to one and despise the other.
You cannot serve God and wealth.*
— Luke 16:13

Help us, Lord Jesus! Our possessions have come to master us. Worldly pleasures have become cruel taskmasters. We need more than flimsy resolve to resist the seductive powers of this age. Call forth even greater love from our hearts. Expose lesser affections as vain and worthless. Fortify our resolve to despise the treasures of this world. Fill us with hope to become all that You have called us to be: those who serve You in love. *Pray:*

- For struggling believers to serve Christ in love without fragmenting their lives with competing ambitions.
- For those far from Christ to be nauseated by worldly enticements and become hungry for the life of God.

Seek God on behalf of **Educators**

That teachers and mentors will impart godly wisdom to help form character in their students; for needed tools and proper facilities; for those who home-school their children; for renewed zeal for truth and virtue; that they would have opportunity to know God in Christ; that believers would know how to pray for their students.

Prayerwalk: As you walk around a school, pray for the teachers, administrators and other staff.

...but everyone who is fully trained will be like his teacher.
— Luke 6:40 (NIV)

Seek God on behalf of **the Americas and the Caribbean**
Puerto Rico, Saint Kitts and Nevis, Saint Lucia, Saint Pierre and Miquelon

Day 10

FRIDAY
FEBRUARY 22

SEEK GOD
...for God to unite His people

How good and pleasant it is when brothers live together in unity!...For there the LORD bestows His blessing, even life forevermore.
– Psalm 133:1, 3 (NIV)

Uniting in worship before You is what we have been made and saved for. There are times when we have worshiped together, and tasted the joy of finally coming home as beloved sons and daughters. But we come to You now as a broken household. Petty differences have shattered friendships in the family of faith. We have ignored, despised and offended one another. Bring us together again. Train us in what is good. Restore what is pleasant. And bring to life the mighty blessing of being together as Your children.

The glory which You have given Me I have given to them, that they may be one...so that the world may know that You sent Me, and loved them, even as You have loved Me.
– John 17:22-23

Lord Jesus, don't give us Your glory without making us one. When we are divided by petty agendas, grudges or hatreds, we become spectacles of foolish arrogance and religious superiority. But when we are fused as one in Your purpose, we can reflect Your glory to all the world. You have loved us and saved us that we may bear Your beauty. Make us one so that the world will know the glorious love of the Father. *Pray:*

- For believers to set aside petty jealousies, repent of sins against each other and be restored to vital unity.
- For divided congregations to become reconciled, reflecting Christ's beauty.
- For churches in your city to work together as never before.

Seek God on behalf of **Health Care Workers**

That God will equip health care workers of every kind to serve others with loving hearts; that God will bless them with perseverance and joy; that the pressure of their professions will not crush their families and friendships; that many will follow Christ.

Prayerwalk: Pray on or near the grounds of a hospital or clinic.

Blessed is he who has regard for the weak; the LORD delivers him in times of trouble. The LORD will protect him and preserve his life; He will bless him in the land.
– Psalm 41:1-2 (NIV)

Seek God on behalf of **the Americas and the Caribbean**

Saint Vincent and the Grenadines, Suriname, Trinidad and Tobago, Turks and Caicos Islands

SEEK GOD
...to bring life from His people to the world

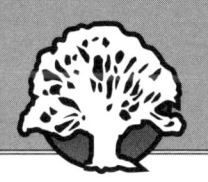

Day 11
SATURDAY
FEBRUARY 23

So everything will live where the river goes...By the river on its bank...will grow all kinds of trees for food. Their leaves will not wither and their fruit will not fail...and their fruit will be for food and their leaves for healing.
— Ezekiel 47:9, 12

You are sending a life-giving river to the world. Your life is already streaming from Your throne, releasing reviving power to us, and then through us to many more. The river may only be ankle deep at this hour. But we anticipate days of grace when nothing will hold back Your life from any place on earth. Unleash the river. Let it flow further than ever before. Remove whatever hinders Your goodness. Flood the nations that have not yet known Your boundless transforming power. Establish Your people everywhere, as if they were feeding, healing trees amidst the nations.

Now on the last day, the great day of the feast, Jesus stood and cried out, saying, "If anyone is thirsty, let him come to Me and drink. He who believes in Me, as the Scripture said, 'From his innermost being will flow rivers of living water.'"
— John 7:37-38

Stand again in our midst, as You did in that day so long ago. Raise Your voice and cry out again so that multitudes will hear. Call us to come to drink deeply of You. Satisfy our deepest yearnings. Fill us to overflowing so that we become life-giving streams to many others. *Pray:*

- That spiritually thirsty people will hear the voice of Christ calling them to Himself.
- For Christians to become conduits of God's life to others.
- For churches to become sources of healing for what is broken in our cities.

Seek God on behalf of **Ministries**

That Christian ministries will be founded on God's truth, anointed by God's power and funded by God's people; for refreshed vision and encouragement upon the dedicated workers who labor in specialized service designed to increase the impact of local churches.

Prayerwalk: Find a high point from which you can see much of the community. Pray that God would send needed Christian workers to your city and at the same time send Christian workers from your city.

Finally, brothers, pray for us that the word of the Lord will spread rapidly and be glorified, just as it did also with you.
— 2 Thessalonians 3:1

Seek God on behalf of **the Americas and the Caribbean**
United States of America, Uruguay, Venezuela, Virgin Islands of the USA

Seeking His **Light**
to Awaken the Lost

FEBRUARY 24 - MARCH 2   WEEK 2

This week we will focus our prayers on those who have yet to follow Christ. We'll be asking God to awaken people from spiritual death. Persuasive words or demonstrations of power and kindness can never be enough to cause people to turn toward God. If people ever come to follow Christ, it is because He draws them to Himself by bringing His light into their darkness.

People are not "lost" to God because they are misdirected or mixed up about religious things. God considers people to be lost when relationship with Him is severed. That's why He loves to hear prayer on their behalf–so that His love will be revealed. Pray in hope that there will be great awakenings to Christ, the Light of the world.

Asia and the Pacific

This week we will extend our prayers for the peoples, cities, churches and families of Asia and the Pacific region.

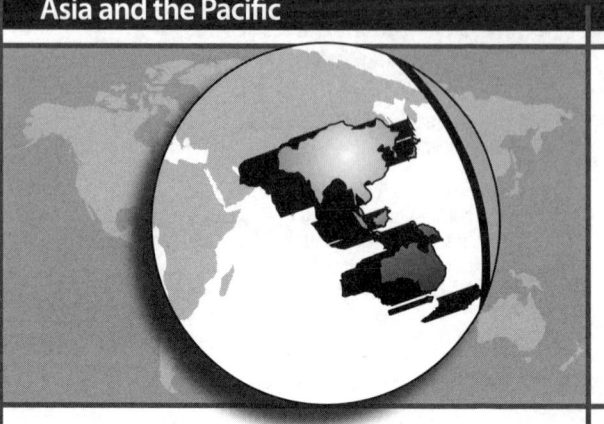

SEEK GOD
...for the light of the gospel to shine

Day 12
SUNDAY
FEBRUARY 24

*The people who walk in darkness
will see a great light.
Those who live in a dark land,
the light will shine on them.*
— Isaiah 9:2

We know the pain of living in the darkness of our hearts, stumbling over our fears, as if it were always night. Lord of light, we plead for our friends who shuffle along through their days, groping with uncertainty, as if they were blind. They have every good intention, but they cannot find their way. And many give up. Some are paralyzed in despair. Just as You did for us, bring light from heaven upon them. There is no way we can throw on a switch for them. There is no candle we can light. Lift the veil and come like the sun upon them.

*Because of the tender mercy of our God,
with which the Sunrise from on high
will visit us, to shine upon those who
sit in darkness and the shadow of death.*
— Luke 1:78-79

You have promised to come like the dawn—slow and steady, but eventually brightening everything. When You came, Lord Jesus, You came like a sunrise, shedding life-giving light on those who were captive to a heavy spiritual darkness. Many could suddenly see and they began to seek You. We ask You now for such an increase of light in our city. We ask You to bring Your visitation upon our entire community like a different kind of dawn—coming not from the east, but instead, coming from above, revealing the tender power of God's love to all.
Pray:

- For Christ's light to shine into the darkened hearts of people you know.
- For God to visit your community, revealing His mercy to many.

Seek God on behalf of **The Poor**

For God to establish the poor so that their spiritual and physical needs are met with dignity and stability; that God will release them from cycles of oppression and despair; that God will reverse every curse and multiply blessing.

Prayerwalk: Walk places of poverty and neglect. Ask the Holy Spirit to give you His eyes and His heart in order to pray from hope, not pity. What grieves or gladdens God as He walks amidst the poor?

*I know that the LORD
will maintain the cause
of the afflicted and justice
for the poor.*
— Psalm 140:12

Seek God on behalf of **Asia and the Pacific**
Afghanistan, American Samoa, Antarctica, Australia, Bangladesh, Bhutan, Brunei, Cambodia

Day 13

MONDAY
FEBRUARY 25

SEEK GOD
...for God's love to be received

Therefore the LORD longs to be gracious to you, and therefore He waits on high to have compassion on you...How blessed are all those who long for Him.
— Isaiah 30:18

We pray for the ones who long ago postponed knowing You. They weren't wicked, but just busy and bothered with stuff that seemed important. Day after squandered day rolled into long, empty years of distraction. They were lightly satisfied with lesser things. And now they find their hearts apathetic, drained of almost all desire to know You. But the desire of Your heart has never changed. You have always watched them, loving them with vast compassion every day of their lives. Now is the time! Wait no longer. Move upon their hearts to reawaken love for You. Reignite their deepest longings so that they will seek You, find You and come to love You—as You have so long desired.

Jesus...said, "What do you want Me to do for you?" They said to Him, "Lord, we want our eyes to be opened." Moved with compassion, Jesus touched their eyes; and immediately they regained their sight and followed Him.
— Matthew 20:32-34

How would our friends answer if You asked them what they wanted from You? They may not know what they truly desire. Keep searching their souls. Find those who are desperate to have their vision restored. Move in Your immense compassion, gently touching them so that their eyes are open to You. Restore the spiritual sight of many throughout our city. Those who see You will follow You. *Pray:*

- For the eyes of the spiritually blind to be opened to recognize God's love.
- That people would experience the amazing compassion of Jesus.

Seek God on behalf of **Refugees**

For safe, legal immigration and for conditions to improve in homelands so that extended families will be united; for Christians to open homes and hearts to them; for the gospel to be conveyed clearly; for those desiring to return to homelands to be granted asylum and repatriation; that God would open the way for those desiring a new home to be resettled.

Prayerwalk: Pray prayers of welcome, protection and blessing for refugees and immigrants in your community.

He defends the cause of the fatherless and the widow, and loves the alien, giving him food and clothing. And you are to love those who are aliens, for you yourselves were aliens in Egypt.
– Deuteronomy 10:18-19 (NIV)

Seek God on behalf of **Asia and the Pacific**
China-People's Republic, China-Taiwan, Christmas Island, Cocos (Keeling) Islands, Cook Islands, Fiji

SEEK GOD
...for the word of God to be understood

Day 14
TUESDAY
FEBRUARY 26

The unfolding of Your words gives light. It gives understanding to the simple.
— Psalm 119:130

We long for Your words to become alive in the hearts of our friends. In fear, pride or folly, some of them have darkened the windows of their lives. Even if they have heard the words before, we ask You to send Your word to them yet again. Give them humility of heart to listen. Send word-bearers who are humble and wise, whose lives match the message. Even a small portion of Your word, when unfolded faithfully, can burst into radiant light. And with Your light bring life.

Then He opened their minds to understand the Scriptures.
— Luke 24:45

Lord Jesus, when You unrolled the scrolls in synagogues, You surprised the crowds by opening the Scriptures like no other. But You did more than merely open the words, You opened the minds of Your followers to understand. Unblock the minds of those who hear Your word today. Pour light upon the pages as they read. Clear away deception so they will comprehend the amazing greatness of what You have done. *Pray:*

- For the word of God to be proclaimed with power and simplicity.
- For the Scriptures to get into the hands of truth seekers in your city.
- For God to illumine His word by the Spirit of God, bringing conviction and clarity.

Seek God on behalf of **Pastors**

That pastors and church leaders will be filled with wisdom; that they will be honored by those they serve; that God will pour His Spirit upon them in power and humility, giving fresh intimacy with Jesus; for protection from the plots of the evil one against their families; that deep friendships with other pastors will grow.

Prayerwalk: Pray outside a church building for the pastor who serves that church.

Be shepherds of God's flock that is under your care...Cast all your anxiety on Him because He cares for you.
— 1 Peter 5:2, 7 (NIV)

Seek God on behalf of **Asia and the Pacific**
French Polynesia, Guam, Hong Kong, India, Indonesia, Japan, Kiribatii

Day 15

WEDNESDAY
FEBRUARY 27

SEEK GOD
...for revelation leading to repentance

*I have heard of You
by the hearing of the ear;
but now my eye sees You.
Therefore I retract,
and I repent in dust and ashes.*
— Job 42:5-6

We pray for those who have heard about You yet remain stone-cold to You. Some have been told that You are the source of their suffering. Others are disappointed that You have not given them quick solutions to their problems. Reveal Yourself in all Your majesty. Vindicate Your reputation by disclosing Your mighty mercy. Allow them to see how their sin has brought incredible sorrow to Your heart. Disclose Your awesome kindness, so that their stony hearts melt in view of how determined You are to love them. Cause them to behold Jesus Himself—in all His excellence and humility. Receive them with joy as they turn to You.

"Who is He, Lord, that I may believe in Him?" Jesus said to him, "You have both seen Him, and He is the one who is talking with you." And he said, "Lord, I believe." And he worshiped Him.
— John 9:36-38

Some of our friends seem cynical or blind to You. But many would trust You if they came to know who You really are. Make Yourself known to them as You have revealed Yourself to millions of others. Show them that You are the same Jesus who acted in the Gospels with eye-opening power. May the spiritually blind come to see. May those who see come to believe. And may those who believe become dedicated worshipers. *Pray:*

- For the hard-hearted to encounter God's love so clearly that they reject false ideas about God.

- For spiritually blind people to see Jesus Christ so that they trust Him and become full-hearted worshipers.

Seek God on behalf of **Prisoners** and their **Families**

That people in jails and prisons will hear the gospel and follow Christ; for fellowships of believers to multiply; that they be protected from violence and forces of spiritual evil; that the spouses and children of prisoners would be sustained, protected, provided for and honored rightly; that released prisoners find strength and wisdom to live abundant lives.

Prayerwalk: Pray near a correctional facility or jail. Or as you prayerwalk your neighborhood, pray for the homes that have family members or loved ones in prison, even if you do not know which homes they may be.

You who seek God, let your heart revive. For the LORD hears the needy, and does not despise His who are prisoners.
— Psalm 69:32-33

Seek God on behalf of **Asia and the Pacific**

Korea-North, Korea-South, Laos, Macau, Malaysia, Maldives, Marshall Islands, Micronesia

SEEK GOD
...to rescue people from spiritual darkness

Day 16
THURSDAY
FEBRUARY 28

There were those who dwelt in darkness and in the shadow of death, prisoners in misery and chains, because they had rebelled against the words of God... Then they cried out to the LORD in their trouble. He saved them... He brought them out of darkness and the shadow of death and broke their bands apart.
— Psalm 107:10-11, 13-14

We pray for many who are locked in lifestyles that hold them in darkness. Some desperately search in vain for escape from the grim misery of their lives. Some feel the chill of death already overshadowing them. Hear their cry, O God. Penetrate prisons locked by pride. Shatter the habits that bind them like chains. Break the bars of resentment and hatred that keep them from authentic relationships of love. Light up the darkness of their lives so they can walk away from the grief of sin and follow You.

Men loved the darkness rather than the Light, for their deeds were evil... But he who practices the truth comes to the Light, so that his deeds may be manifested as having been wrought in God.
— John 3:19, 21

You have dispelled the darkness in countless lives, yet many continue to be enslaved in the ways they have chosen. Make them weary of hiding in the shadows of habitual sin. Energize them by the mighty power of grace to take even one step toward the light of Your truth. And after that first step, give them another, and then another, until they find themselves attracted by the bright hope that they shall be changed. *Pray:*

- For God to subdue powers of evil that hold people in darkness.
- For the light of the gospel to expose what is false and to illumine the hope of freedom in Jesus.
- That new believers will put the truth they know into daily practice.

Seek God on behalf of **Men**

That men will seek God and honor Him in faithfulness, wisdom and truth; for their identity to be centered in Christ-like servant leadership; that the vision of their lives would be to serve and advance God's purposes.

Prayerwalk: You will see many men today. Ask God to help you focus your prayers on one or two.

Let not the wise man boast of his wisdom or the strong man boast of his strength or the rich man boast of his riches, but let him who boasts boast about this: that he understands and knows Me.
— Jeremiah 9:23-24 (NIV)

Seek God on behalf of **Asia and the Pacific**

Mongolia, Myanmar, Nauru, Nepal, New Caledonia, New Zealand, Niue, Norfolk Island

Day 17
FRIDAY MARCH 1

SEEK GOD
...for God to free people from powers of darkness

The LORD will go forth like a warrior, He will arouse His zeal like a man of war. He will utter a shout, yes, He will raise a war cry. He will prevail against His enemies..."I will lead the blind by a way they do not know. In paths they do not know I will guide them. I will make darkness into light before them..."
– Isaiah 42:13, 16

Come, awesome God of power. Hear our cry for help. Arouse Yourself as a champion warrior to overwhelm the spiritual powers that hold millions captive in our land. Raise Your mighty voice, a mighty shout of war, scattering the powers of darkness. And yet call out clearly as a tender shepherd to those who are oppressed or lost. Lead many to freedom, like a herdsman bringing his flock homeward. Fight this war in ways that we cannot. Lead us in ways of freedom that we will never discover on our own. Prevail over evil so decisively that our darkness is turned to Your light.

Now judgment is upon this world; now the ruler of this world will be cast out. And I, if I am lifted up from the earth, will draw all men to Myself...While you have the Light, believe in the Light, so that you may become sons of Light.
– John 12:31-32, 36

You triumphed over satanic power by Your death on the cross. You did not die to merely conquer the evil one. You died to bring people back into relationship with You. We cannot celebrate Your victory over Satan unless You accomplish Your purpose of drawing many to Yourself. Now is the time. Lift the light of Your glory among the people of our city. Cause them to come to You and become children of light who reflect Your glory. *Pray:*

- That God would deliver those troubled by demonic powers in your city.
- That God would liberate friends who are trapped in cults or the occult.
- For believers to live as sons and daughters of light.

Seek God on behalf of **Physically Disabled People**

That they will be surrounded with loving friends and family; for steady refreshment of their hearts toward God; for physical stamina and healing; for financial provision to cover the cost of therapy and special care; that they will know and display the love of God.

Prayerwalk: Pray along the same route that a person with disabilities might use to move through your neighborhood, school or workplace. As you do, pray for someone you know with disabilities.

In all their affliction He was afflicted...In His love and in His mercy He redeemed them, and He lifted them and carried them all the days of old.
– Isaiah 63:9

Seek God on behalf of **Asia and the Pacific**
Northern Mariana Islands, Pakistan, Palau, Papua New Guinea, Philippines, Samoa, Singapore, Solomon Islands

SEEK GOD
...for God's light to bring abundant life

Day 18
SATURDAY
MARCH 2

How precious is Your lovingkindness, O God! And the children of men take refuge in the shadow of Your wings. They drink their fill of the abundance of Your house; and You give them to drink of the river of Your delights. For with You is the fountain of life. In Your light we see light.
— Psalm 36:7-9

From Your house there flows a river, a stream of steady love. Give our friends a taste of that love. Many keep themselves far from You. They are sure that You are angry with them, despising and punishing them. So they have wandered in the shadows where they think You cannot find them. Let them experience Your joy—the joy of Your heart when Your children simply love You. If You give them even a small sip of the fountain of Your favor, they will be drawn near to drink their fill. Overshadow them with the warmth of Your love and bring them all the way home.

Then Jesus again spoke to them, saying, "I am the Light of the world; he who follows Me will not walk in the darkness, but will have the Light of life."
— John 8:12

Jesus, light of the world, give our friends who walk in darkness more than a glimpse of your life-changing light. Call them to follow You. By walking with You, Your light will reach inside them with healing and transforming power. Shine even brighter throughout our community so that many will be changed by walking in Your light. Pray:

- For people to experience Christ as living light, exposing darkness and imparting wisdom to live like Him.
- For the light of the gospel to bring many people alive in Christ.

Seek God on behalf of **Mothers**

That God will powerfully refresh mothers in the honor and glory of motherhood; that they will be strengthened with grace, wisdom and love in serving their children; that they will be loved, protected and served by committed husbands; that mothers will model and express God's own nurturing love.

Prayerwalk: Walk through your neighborhood, praying for mothers and grandmothers.

She is clothed with strength and dignity; she can laugh at the days to come. She speaks with wisdom...Her children arise and call her blessed; her husband also, and he praises her.
— Proverbs 31:25-26, 28 (NIV)

Seek God on behalf of **Asia and the Pacific**

Sri Lanka, Thailand, Tibet, Timor, Tonga, Tuvalu, Vanuatu, Vietnam, Wallis and Futuna, West Papua (Irian Jaya)

Seeking His **Glory** in Evangelizing All Peoples

MARCH 3-9 WEEK 3

As God works by the power of the gospel, people are transformed by Christ. Their families and communities begin to change and God is increasingly thanked for His goodness. God receives more glory as people grow into the image of Christ and offer God explicit worship by His Spirit.

This week we are praying for every people group to be evangelized. We aren't overreaching as we focus on the glory Christ will gain for the Father in a thoroughly evangelized world. Such hope is clearly promised in Scripture. God has been moving in tremendous ways in many parts of the world. Now is the time to pray that God will move even more powerfully so that He will be glorified by a movement of loving obedience in every people throughout the communities of the world.

Africa

This week we will be praying for the cities, peoples, tribes and countries of the continent of Africa.

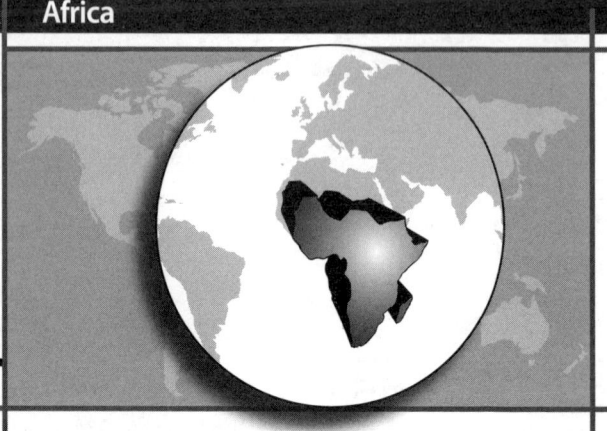

SEEK GOD
...for His renown among all peoples

Day 19
SUNDAY
MARCH 3

Give thanks to the LORD, call on His name. Make known His deeds among the peoples. Make them remember that His name is exalted...He has done excellent things. Let this be known throughout the earth.
– Isaiah 12:4-5

At this moment, people are praising You on the other side of the planet. Yet You are not praised on the other side of our city. For too long You have gone anonymous in our community. Because people do not know You, they consider the good things You do for them to be luck or coincidence. Kindness is considered a random thing. You are denied by the ignorant and defied by the belligerent. Lord of glory, do something great for Your name. Become famous for who You really are. Re-establish Your reputation among those who have forgotten You. Stir Your people to tell the story of Your glory in their lives.

When you pray, say: "Father, hallowed be Your name."
– Luke 11:2

Jesus, You were jealous for Your Father's glory. Everything You did and prayed was intended to reveal the singular beauty of the Father's heart. Show us how to pray for His renown. Bolster our courage so that we pray large enough to match the great things the Father longs to do in our community. May the marvels of the Father's love soon become known and celebrated among those who have never experienced His love. *Pray:*

- For believers to become story-tellers, recounting what God has done in their lives.
- That God will reveal Himself to people who have denied or defied Him.
- For God to be thanked for doing great things in your community.

Seek God on behalf of **Government Leaders**

That they will be examples of righteousness to our society; that they will experience God's wisdom in their deliberations; that they will speak and carry out dealings with truth; that they will not hinder the service and worship of Jesus Christ; that they will come to know, honor and follow Christ.

Prayerwalk: Visit a center of city, state or federal government. Pray on or near the site. Leave a short note for a particular official which describes your prayers for God to bless them.

I urge, then, first of all, that requests, prayers, intercession and thanksgiving be made for everyone—for kings and all those in authority.
– 1 Timothy 2:1-2 (NIV)

Seek God on behalf of **Africa**
Angola, Benin, Botswana, Burkina Faso, Burundi, Cameroon, Cape Verde Islands

Day 20

MONDAY
MARCH 4

SEEK GOD
...that His people would reflect His great name

Do something for the sake of Your name. For our backsliding is great; we have sinned against You... Why are You like a stranger in the land, like a traveler who stays only a night? Why are You like a man taken by surprise, like a warrior powerless to save? You are among us, O LORD, and we bear Your name; do not forsake us!
— Jeremiah 14:7-9 (NIV)

Our sin has degraded Your reputation. We are ashamed that we have dishonored Your name. Because of our backsliding, our doubt and our self-reliance, many have concluded that You are not to be trusted. You have become a bygone memory, a phantom of the past. Some speak of You as a vicious tyrant. Others regard You as aloof and uncaring. Forgive us. We beg You to vindicate Your name. You are wise, mighty and good. Become great again in our sight and glorious among the nations.

"Father, glorify Your name." Then a voice came out of heaven: "I have both glorified it, and will glorify it again." — John 12:28

Our Father, we echo this, the prayer of Your Son, that Your renown would be greater than ever in these days. You glorified Yourself in Jesus. Now, as You have promised, glorify Your name yet again. If You are known truly, then You can be followed fully. Father, glorify Your name! *Pray:*

- For backslidden Christians to become faithful, God-honoring Christ followers.
- For false ideas about God to be exposed and for the truth of God to be reflected in the lives of Christians.
- That double-minded Christians would turn to God in repentance and reflect His glory.

Seek God on behalf of **News Media**

For people throughout the industries of broadcast and print media to come to know Jesus personally; that attitudes of cynicism will be changed; for those who love Christ to be strengthened in wisdom; for a growing emphasis in their work on that which carries virtue and conveys kingdom values throughout the city.

Prayerwalk: Visit a media center, a broadcast station or a publisher of print media. Pray for some of those who are associated with that particular enterprise.

These are the things which you should do: speak the truth to one another; judge with truth and judgment for peace in your gates.
— Zechariah 8:16

Seek God on behalf of **Africa**
Central African Republic, Chad, Comoros, Congo-Democratic Republic (Zaire), Cote d'Ivoire, Djiboutii

SEEK GOD
...to display His love and power by answered prayer

Day 21
TUESDAY
MARCH 5

Hear in heaven Your dwelling place, and do according to all for which the foreigner calls to You, in order that all the peoples of the earth may know Your name, to fear You, as do Your people. – 1 Kings 8:43

Hear and answer when lost people pray so that You will be glorified in their sight. Have mercy and hear them no matter how stubbornly they may have fought You or how far they may have fled from You. Hear their desperation with Your perfect wisdom. Be moved by their sorrows with Your boundless compassion. Hear their cry. Act swiftly, responding to the weakest whisper of prayer. Demonstrate Your power, win their praise and call them to Your kingdom.

They were all struck with astonishment and began glorifying God; and they were filled with fear, saying, "We have seen remarkable things today." – Luke 5:26

Lord Jesus, we ask you to work today in the same remarkable ways as You worked on earth so long ago. You responded with compassion to the faith of ordinary people as they brought their friends and family members to You. As you prayed, God worked with such astounding power that reports rippled throughout entire communities. And so today we ask You to honor the faith of ordinary people who cry out to You. Demonstrate the loving power of the living God so decisively that people will openly exclaim His praise. *Pray:*

- For Christians to pray for others in wise and sensitive ways.
- For God to hear and to answer the prayers of people who do not yet know Christ.
- For desperate people to cry out to God for help.

Seek God on behalf of **Homeless People**

That God brings immediate relief, shelter, food and health care; that Christ will restore hope for the future; for wise counsel and trustworthy friendship; for protection from the risks of life on the streets; for employment, housing and restored family life.

Prayerwalk: Visit a place where homeless people seek shelter or employment. Pray God's blessing on the people you see who appear to be homeless.

But He lifted the needy out of their affliction and increased their families like flocks.
– Psalm 107:41 (NIV)

Seek God on behalf of **Africa**
Equatorial Guinea, Eritrea, Ethiopia, Gabon, The Gambia, Ghana, Guinea, Guinea Bissau

Day 22
WEDNESDAY MARCH 6

SEEK GOD
...to be recognized and honored by leaders

O kings, show discernment; take warning, O judges of the earth. Worship the LORD with reverence and rejoice with trembling...How blessed are all who take refuge in Him!
— Psalm 2:10-12

We pray for the leaders of our land. The same forces that exalted them to power could just as quickly turn on them. Their precarious positions are as permanent as sand castles. But angry voters and hostile armies are not their greatest danger. They stand before You, Almighty God, accountable for all their deeds. Because they govern Your little ones and make decisions concerning justice, they will answer to You for every choice and word. And so we pray that they would submit their governance to Your greater wisdom. Give them hope in Your majesty as Judge of all the earth. May they come to honor You openly. And as they find true refuge in You, protect and encourage them. Bless the cities and lands they lead for Your glory.

"When you have found Him, report to me, so that I too may come and worship Him." After hearing the king, they went their way...When they saw the star, they rejoiced exceedingly with great joy. After coming into the house... they fell to the ground and worshiped Him.
— Matthew 2:8-11

Lord Jesus, guide our leaders to give You glory. Governing leaders are still drawn to You for all the reasons they searched for You at Your birth. Some are threatened by Your coming kingship and try to oppose You, as if they could rival Your majesty. Others wisely rejoice to welcome Your coming kingdom. Reveal Yourself so that leaders honor You as the only one worthy of the worship in all the earth. *Pray:*

- That government leaders who fear God would openly express reverence and honor for Jesus Christ.
- For local, state and national officials to know the truth of Christ and His kingdom.

Seek God on behalf of **Business People**

Ask God to bless those who base business practices in righteousness. Pray that God will prosper those who pursue their business as mission for God's kingdom. Pray for the gospel to spread in the marketplace; for righteous managers and executives; for creative, godly entrepreneurs. Pray that God would frustrate plans which escalate injustice.

Prayerwalk: As you pass through a place of business today, pray for Christ to be followed and for His name to be honored in that setting. Pray for God to bless all that expresses His kingdom.

But remember the LORD your God, for it is He who gives you the ability to produce wealth.
— Deuteronomy 8:18 (NIV)

Seek God on behalf of **Africa**
Kenya, Lesotho, Liberia, Madagascar, Malawi, Mali, Mauritania, Mauritius

SEEK GOD
...for every people group to hear the gospel

Day 23
THURSDAY
MARCH 7

Sing to the LORD, all the earth. Proclaim good tidings of His salvation from day to day. Tell of His glory among the nations, His wonderful deeds among all the peoples.
— 1 Chronicles 16:23-24

May the word of Your kingdom be announced with such winsome clarity that all the peoples of the earth will hear of Your salvation. You have brought people from distant nations to the cities of our land, but many are still far from You. Send Your people to convey the gospel with persuasive beauty and disarming kindness. Send Your word out with a song, so that the sweet reality of Your love seeps into the souls of those who hear. May Your love be told as an epic story so that people are amazed by the beauty of what You've done for them. Let Your story be told again and again, until every people on earth and every group of our city has heard the story of Your glory.

"Return to your house and describe what great things God has done for you." So he went away, proclaiming throughout the whole city what great things Jesus had done for him.
— Luke 8:39

One man reported to his own people the things You did for him. The news went beyond his household so that the whole city heard. Do the same thing in our city. May one relay the gospel to another, and then throughout their households. Resound the word through neighborhoods and networks of friends. Fill our entire community with fresh tellings of the gospel. And from our city, send the message to every people and place on earth. *Pray:*

- For believers to become storytellers, eagerly communicating the gospel to every ethnicity of your community.
- For the gospel to be conveyed powerfully with heart-stirring music.
- For new believers to tell the people closest to them about Jesus.

Seek God on behalf of **University Students**

Pray for evangelization of entire campuses; for many to follow Christ; for the truth to radiate in a setting often hostile and cynical toward matters of faith; for students to make wise decisions, to form godly lifestyles and to shape their careers and ambitions to fulfill God's global purposes. Pray for leadership to be strong among Christian groups on campuses; for the advance of movements of prayer and mission mobilization; for the ministries that focus on students.

Prayerwalk: Pray for students at a place of higher education.

Study to shew thyself approved unto God, a workman that needeth not to be ashamed.
— 2 Timothy 2:15 (KJV)

Seek God on behalf of **Africa**
Mayotte, Mozambique, Namibia, Niger, Nigeria, Republic of Congo, Réunion

Day 24
FRIDAY
MARCH 8

SEEK GOD
...that many would know and follow Him

Many peoples and the inhabitants of many cities will yet come, and the inhabitants of one city will go to another and say, "Let us go at once to entreat the LORD and seek the LORD Almighty. I myself am going." And many peoples and powerful nations will come.
— Zechariah 8:20-22 (NIV)

We have heard of great movements to Christ in far-off places of the earth. Chain reactions of faith are drawing many thousands to You every day. First a family, then a clan and then many throughout entire peoples suddenly surge toward Christ. Yet we have been content with a few people visiting our churches. Our hearts know better. Your hopes are greater. You have promised that great movements of people will rise to seek and to know You. Let our community be among those that will stimulate such movements of people who will love and follow Christ.

Look how the whole world has gone after Him! — John 12:19 (NIV)

No one calls forth movements like You, Lord Jesus. During the three short years before Your resurrection, great throngs sought You in the cities. Crowds found You in the countryside. Leaders came to You in secret. Even Your enemies said that it seemed like the whole world was coming to You. And it continues to this day. People in many parts of the earth are following You as never before. We pray for our city and land, that You would call forth tremendous movements of inquiry, repentance and faith. Train many to become faithful followers who will draw even more to seek You.
Pray:

- For the Holy Spirit to set the hearts of many to seek and to know Jesus.
- For disciple-making laborers to be raised up to serve and sustain new Christward movements.

Seek God on behalf of **Native Peoples**

For God's fullest blessing upon Native Americans; that those who live in or near your city would be honored for who they are and for all God intends them to be; that God would heal the wounds to our nation that have resulted from broken treaties and mistreatment; that the tribes will be treated justly and find their destiny and highest dignity; that churches will flourish among them and that God's praise will resound in first nation languages.

Prayerwalk: As you prayerwalk, consider the native peoples who first dwelt in the area that has become your city. Pray for their descendents.

Let the nations be glad and sing for joy; for You will judge the peoples with uprightness and guide the nations on the earth.
— Psalm 67:4

Seek God on behalf of **Africa**
Rwanda, Saint Helena, Sao Tome and Principe, Senegal, Seychelles, Sierra Leone, Somalia, South Africa

SEEK GOD

...for God to be worshiped by all peoples

Day 25
SATURDAY
MARCH 9

All nations whom You have made shall come and worship before You, O Lord, and they shall glorify Your name. For You are great and do wondrous deeds; You alone are God. – Psalm 86:9-10

But an hour is coming, and now is, when the true worshipers will worship the Father in spirit and truth; for such people the Father seeks to be His worshipers. – John 4:23

You have set Your heart to call forth a worshiping people from every land and language. The sullen, secular dullness of our day can make such promises seem like impossible fantasies. We lift our eyes to You, Lord Jesus. With Your own blood You have purchased some from every people. By Your resurrection power You have done wondrous deeds throughout the generations. How can the Father's purpose fail? The coming extravaganza of worshipers is a future fact, more sure than today's newspaper. And so we pray with confidence: Complete what You have begun! We dare ask that You would surpass Yourself in our day. We pray for You to exhibit even greater deeds of healing and renewal. Become famous for transforming lives of every kind. Gather willing worshipers from the diverse peoples in our city. May Your praise resound in all the earth.

We do not have to persuade You to seek worshipers. You have yearned to be worshiped with a passion that is ancient, vast and forceful, beyond human description. It is right for us to plead that Your love would be answered by love-filled worship from all peoples. Now is the hour. Search our city and find the devoted worshipers You have so long desired. *Pray:*

- For a wave of new mission workers to be sent, filled with the Father's zeal for the nations.
- For worship leaders in your city to be focused on biblical truth and filled with God's Spirit.
- For Christ-centered worship to emerge in every ethnic community of your city.

Seek God on behalf of **Judges and Law Enforcement**

Pray for righteous wisdom, principled patience and gentle authority; for physical and emotional protection; for strength and blessing for their families; that they will become agents of God's hand to resist evil and preserve an environment in which heaven's justice can increase.

Prayerwalk: Pray outside the nearest police station or court. Leave a short personal note for judges or police leaders letting them know how Christians are praying for them today.

Blessed are they who maintain justice, who constantly do what is right.
– Psalm 106:3 (NIV)

Seek God on behalf of **Africa**
South Sudan, Sudan, Swaziland, Tanzania, Togo, Uganda, Western Sahara, Zambia, Zimbabwe

Seeking His **Righteousness** in Our Communities

MARCH 10-16 WEEK 4

Righteousness is sometimes misunderstood as merely being right. But righteousness has nothing to do with religious superiority. It is simply life rightly lived in God's sight. Because of Christ's life and power, broken people can be changed to live in Christ's righteousness.

God has purposed to bring about much more than personal righteousness. The kingdom of God is marked by peace, joy and righteousness lived out in everyday life (Romans 14:17). He wants to change the lives of many people at once so that the righteous character of Christ is on display throughout entire communities.

Europe and Central Asia

This fourth week we will direct our prayers with and for the people, churches and countries of Europe and Central Asia.

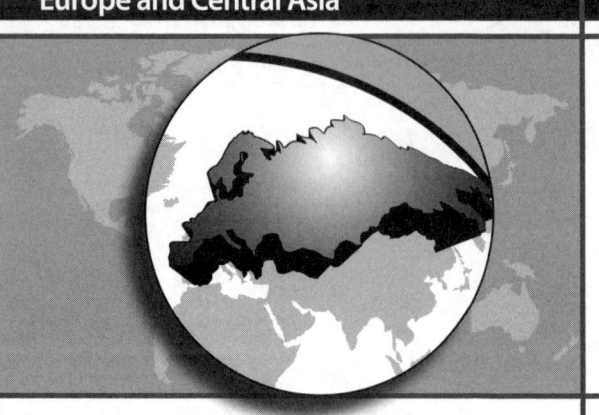

SEEK GOD
...to bring blessing through righteousness

Day 26
SUNDAY
MARCH 10

Abraham will surely become a great and mighty nation, and in him all the nations of the earth will be blessed... For I have chosen him, so that he may command his children...after him to keep the way of the LORD by doing righteousness and justice, so that the LORD may bring upon Abraham what He has spoken about him.
— Genesis 18:18-19

As Abraham was praying for the city of Sodom, You disclosed Your ways to him: Because of the righteousness of a few, You would show mercy and blessing on many. We approach You now as Abraham's children by faith, that You would have mercy and bring blessing on our community. We cannot claim to have fully lived out the righteousness of Christ. We have yet to practice justice in all our dealings. Do more than forgive us. Reform us and train us to be the righteous people that You have long desired. As You transform our lives in Christ's righteousness, even though we are few, bring about some of the great, long-promised blessing upon our entire city.

...for in this way it is fitting for us to fulfill all righteousness.
— Matthew 3:15

Lord Jesus, when You stepped forward to be baptized, You were not seeking to be made righteous. You had lived perfectly and had no need to be washed clean. Instead, You were seeking to fulfill a larger purpose, that many would be transformed by Your life in order to live right lives. Fulfill what You began. Make many people righteous in God's sight as they follow You and become joined by faith with You. May their lives become a spectacle of Your character, justice and truth. *Pray:*

- For specific people by name, that they would soon trust and follow Christ, and live right lives by His power.
- That justice would be pursued by Christians in your city.

Seek God on behalf of **Unemployed People**

That God will meet the needs of those without work in a way that they can clearly thank God for His provision; that they will soon find meaningful employment and glorify God for it; that God will open the way for righteous trade so that the entire city prospers in His provision.

Prayerwalk: Pray for those in your neighborhood who have recently lost their job or are struggling to find one.

That everyone may eat and drink, and find satisfaction in all his toil—this is the gift of God.
— Ecclesiastes 3:13 (NIV)

Seek God on behalf of **Europe and Central Asia**
Albania, Andorra, Armenia, Austria, Azerbaijan, Belarus, Belgium, Bosnia and Herzegovina, Bulgaria

Day 27

MONDAY
MARCH 11

SEEK GOD
...to intervene to bring forth justice

*Arise, O LORD, in Your anger...
O let the evil of the wicked come
to an end, but establish the righteous.
For the righteous God tries the hearts
and minds...God is a righteous judge,
and a God who has indignation
every day.* — Psalm 7:6, 9, 11

You smolder with rage every single day as You behold acts of cruelty and injustice by those who exploit the weak, abuse the young or crush the poor. Arise, O Judge of all the earth! We cry out for justice, not because we are righteous, but because You are righteous, merciful and good. We call on You to intervene in the lives and affairs of our city. Establish Your righteousness by transforming people to become like You. Reshape our minds to value Your goodness. Penetrate our hearts with Your compassion.

Will not God bring about justice for His chosen ones, who cry out to Him day and night? Will He keep putting them off? I tell you, He will see that they get justice, and quickly. However, when the Son of Man comes, will He find faith on the earth?
— Luke 18:7-8 (NIV)

We must answer "Yes," to Your question. You will indeed find faith on the earth. You will find people praying for You to overturn the works of darkness. We dare now to approach Your court to present our case so that You would overrule the evil that abuses many of our city—even if we must come with the same appeal again and again. When You come back again, we want to be among those who never gave up asking You to bring forth a display of Your justice within the days of history. *Pray:*

- For God to overturn the status quo where there is injustice and entrenched evil.
- For the laws of the land to be framed upon God's standards of righteousness.

Seek God on behalf of **Children**

That children will hear the gospel and encounter Christ early in life; that God's great fatherly heart will be revealed with healing power to kids who have been wounded or disappointed by their parents; for lasting family stability; for excellence in education; for wisdom to be formed in their early days; for safety from violence and perversion; for laughter and joy.

Let the little children come to Me, and do not hinder them, for the kingdom of God belongs to such as these.
— Mark 10:14 (NIV)

Prayerwalk: Pray for kids in your neighborhood or pray near schools and playgrounds in any part of town. Pray for the entire family that surrounds each one of the children that you see.

Seek God on behalf of **Europe and Central Asia**

Canary Islands, Croatia, Czech Republic, Denmark, Estonia, Faeroe Islands, Finland

SEEK GOD
...to inspire a yearning for righteousness

Day 28
TUESDAY
MARCH 12

Indeed, while following the way of Your judgments, O LORD, we have waited for You eagerly; Your name, even Your memory, is the desire of our souls. ...Indeed, my spirit within me seeks You diligently; for when the earth experiences Your judgments the inhabitants of the world learn righteousness. – Isaiah 26:8-9

In these drastic days Your dealings are as mysterious as they are magnificent. We watch and wait in hope for You to vindicate Your name. Though darkness appears to prevail, You will not fail to bring Your kingly rule on the earth. We pray on behalf of those who blindly pursue evil. Extend Your mercy to them by revealing the excellence of Your wisdom and the beauty of Your righteousness. May many of our city welcome Your Lordship.

Blessed are those who hunger and thirst for righteousness, for they shall be satisfied. – Matthew 5:6

Lord Jesus, we rightly celebrate Your perfect sinlessness. But Your righteousness was more than a flawless performance. You aligned Your every thought and emotion with the character of Your Father God. Your words, Your deeds, Your prayers–everything about Your life was lived in consummate fullness. Observing Your life awakens hunger in us to be like You. Give us the gift of desiring righteousness. Instill this desire deep within us, as powerful as thirst. Fill us with hope to see the righteousness of God flourish in our city. *Pray:*

- For God to free people from the hypnotic delusions of sin to see the joy of living in the virtues of Christ's life.
- For God to awaken an appetite to live in His righteousness in Christ-like fullness.

Seek God on behalf of **Substance Abusers**

That God will break every form of bondage, including alcoholism and drug addiction. Pray for wise counselors to bring intervention and help; that God will heal their minds and bodies; that they will turn from self-centeredness to living their lives for Christ.

Prayerwalk: Walk your neighborhood, considering those who may be bound in alcoholism or drug addiction, calling on God to free them.

On the day the LORD gives you relief from suffering and turmoil and cruel bondage.
– Isaiah 14:3 (NIV)

Seek God on behalf of **Europe and Central Asia**
France, Georgia, Germany, Gibraltar, Greece, Hungary, Iceland, Ireland

Day 29
WEDNESDAY MARCH 13

SEEK GOD
...for His Spirit to empower His people

The Spirit of the Lord GOD is upon me... To proclaim the favorable year of the LORD...So they will be called oaks of righteousness, the planting of the LORD, that He may be glorified.
Then they will rebuild the ancient ruins. They will raise up the former devastations; and they will repair the ruined cities, the desolations of many generations.
— Isaiah 61:1-4

"The Spirit of the Lord is upon Me, because He anointed Me to preach the Gospel to the poor. He has sent Me to proclaim release to the captives, and recovery of sight to the blind, to set free those who are oppressed, to proclaim the favorable year of the Lord." ...And He began to say to them, "Today this Scripture has been fulfilled in your hearing." — Luke 4:18-19, 21

Send Your Spirit upon Your people. Plant seeds of hope in the hearts of the downcast. Cause them to grow quickly and spread widely, implanting righteousness where there was none. Raise them up to rebuild devastated communities, even those considered dead for many generations. The remade city does not consist of steel beams or sleek glass. The city You are creating is alive and powerful with righteous life, renewed from within, growing slow and strong like a forest of solid oaks. Come upon us Spirit of God. Bring the promised time of favor for our city.

The Spirit of the Lord is still upon You, Anointed One. Because You live with resurrected power, the same "year of favor" continues to this very day. Push this promise to even greater fulfillment in this hour. Pour Your Spirit upon all of Your people. Extend favor upon entire communities, giving many the opportunity to hear Your word, to see Your love and to be lifted from all that binds them. *Pray:*

- That God will empower Christians to restore and bless your community by His Spirit.
- For many to experience God's favor.

Seek God on behalf of **Depressed People**

That God's healing presence will reach them; that the light of truth will dispel lies and the oppressive power of Satan; for helpful counsel; for the healing of long-standing wounds of mind and soul; that they would know the comfort and joy of the Holy Spirit; for the renewing of their minds in Christ.

Prayerwalk: Pray for people you see today who may be downcast, even though they appear to be cheerful and strong.

But God, who comforts the downcast, comforted us.
— 2 Corinthians 7:6 (NIV)

Seek God on behalf of **Europe and Central Asia**
Italy, Kazakhstan, Kosovo, Kyrgyzstan, Latvia, Liechtenstein, Lithuania, Luxembourg

SEEK GOD
...for freedom from terror

Day 30
THURSDAY
MARCH 14

In righteousness you will be established. You will be far from oppression, for you will not fear; and from terror, for it will not come near you. – Isaiah 54:14

The threat of terror has exploded randomly in so many places, that it seems as if there is no hope of abiding safety. Because lawlessness seems to prevail, and authorities seem powerless to protect, it is difficult to trust. Easy, open-hearted love for others grows cold. Come Prince of Peace! Establish Your people in righteousness. Liberate Your people from the paralyzing terror of our times. Give many people renewed hope of civil city life under the influence of Your Lordship. As Your people obey You by loving neighbors and even enemies, may our kindness become contagious. Because of the rock of Your righteousness, cause friendship to overcome fear.

To grant us that we, being rescued from the hand of our enemies, might serve Him without fear, in holiness and righteousness before Him all our days. – Luke 1:74-75

Give Your people in our city a way to live uprightly for Your glory in wide-open, public ways. We have presumed that persecution is long ago or far away. We refuse to rescue ourselves. It is Yours to save. It is ours to serve. Establish Your people in the safety of following Christ in the virtue of His righteousness. Do not give us the beauty of His holiness apart from the vulnerability of His suffering. Grant Your people a way to worship and serve You fearlessly in the midst of reprisals so that Christ will be glorified. *Pray:*

- For plans of terrorism toward your city to be exposed and thwarted.
- For believers to live free from fear and to become peace-bearers in your city.
- For churches and believers worldwide to be delivered from persecution.

Seek God on behalf of **Fathers**

That fathers will look to God as the ultimate spiritual head of their household, serving and caring for their families; that God will instill a vision for wholesome, supportive fatherhood among the fathers of the city; that absentee fathers would change their lifestyles to nurture their wives and children; that children will see the character of the heavenly Father in the lives of their dads.

Prayerwalk: Pray for the fathers in your workplace or near your home.

Fathers, do not exasperate your children; instead, bring them up in the training and instruction of the Lord.
– Ephesians 6:4 (NIV)

Seek God on behalf of **Europe and Central Asia**
Macedonia, Malta, Moldova, Monaco, Montenegro, Netherlands, Norway, Poland, Portugal

45

Day 31
FRIDAY
MARCH 15

SEEK GOD
...to establish righteous leaders

Then I will restore your judges as at the first, and your counselors as at the beginning; after that you will be called the city of righteousness, a faithful city.
— Isaiah 1:26

The hearts of our leaders are known to You. You know how they have yearned for good things. You recognize their motives to do what seems right. But You also know how they may have been tempted. You see how they may have been compromised. We pray that You would renew their hope and restore their courage. Purify their motives and give them strength to do the right things for all of the right reasons. Increase the influence of those who deal justly. May our community become notorious for righteous and wise leaders. May it be acclaimed as a place of faithfulness.

"Do not judge according to appearance, but judge with righteous judgment."
— John 7:24

Lord Jesus, our leaders are under constant pressure to please different groups and agendas. To maintain their influence, they are tempted to tell white lies that aren't clearly false, but aren't really true. We ask You, God of truth, to fill them with the fear of God. Free them from political demands that cause them to pretend to be someone they are not. Give them confidence in Your ways, so that they will act according to Your righteousness. *Pray:*

- For business leaders to shape their goals in light of God's righteousness.
- For judges, court officials and lawmakers to fear God.
- For corruption to be purged from our justice system.

Seek God on behalf of **Agricultural Workers**

That God will abundantly bless families who farm, ranch or support agricultural industries; that they would follow Christ and find ways to be part of life-giving churches. Pray especially for migrant workers who sometimes face injustice and great difficulties.

Prayerwalk: Pray in a rural area for God's blessing on the land and the families He has placed there.

For the LORD your God will bless you in all your harvest and in all the work of your hands, and your joy will be complete.
— Deuteronomy 16:15 (NIV)

Seek God on behalf of **Europe and Central Asia**
Romania, Russia, San Marino, Serbia, Slovakia, Slovenia, Spain, Sweden

SEEK GOD
...for city-wide righteousness

Day 32
SATURDAY
MARCH 16

Sow with a view to righteousness, reap in accordance with kindness. Break up your fallow ground, for it is time to seek the LORD until He comes to rain righteousness on you.
— Hosea 10:12

How long until we see the harvest of transformation? For years Christians have served our city and often helped the poor. As we have done so, we have envisioned tremendous moves of God. But after we've done what we can, our city seems only slightly improved. Come to us, living God. Visit our city with life from heaven, like a slow, steady rainfall. Cause our caring deeds to be as seeds that sprout to life and bear lasting fruit. Manifest Your presence in our small acts of kindness, so that people seek You eagerly. Bring forth long seasons of city-wide righteousness.

But seek first His kingdom and His righteousness, and all these things will be added to you. — Matthew 6:33

As individual believers, we have gladly received Your Lordship and stand before the living God in the righteousness of Christ. But we want more than merely being right with You in a personal way. We desire Your kingdom throughout our city. Surely Your jurisdiction extends to all the streets and homes and businesses of our community. Bring displays of Your righteousness in our society. We want Your kingdom to come so that Your will is actually done in the affairs of business, education and governance.
Pray:

- For believers in your city to seek God's kingdom above all other things.
- For Christ's Lordship to change people in both private matters as well as public affairs.

Seek God on behalf of **Arts and Entertainment**

That God will inspire artists and those in the entertainment industry with creativity and wisdom that reflect God's beauty; that they will seek God themselves and come to follow Christ with courage; that their work will bring strength, goodness and hope to our communities.

Prayerwalk: Visit a theater, art museum or place of entertainment for the purpose of praying for the artists and those working in support capacities.

He has filled him with the Spirit of God, with skill, ability and knowledge in all kinds of crafts... to engage in all kinds of artistic craftsmanship.
— Exodus 35:31, 33 (NIV)

Seek God on behalf of **Europe and Central Asia**
Switzerland, Tajikistan, Turkmenistan, Ukraine, United Kingdom, Uzbekistan, Vatican City

Seeking His **Peace**
Among All Peoples

MARCH 17-23 WEEK 5

Jesus did not promise that peace would prevail in this age. He actually assured us that there would be great conflicts until the end. Nevertheless, it is always right to pray for God to bring peace.

God's peace is not absence of war, it is the infusion of heaven's life on earth. It's what love looks like when many people walk in God's ways and live in His power. Although peace won't prevail in this age, we can be sure that Christ is creating outbreaks of heaven's peace in every community as a sign that His kingdom is on the way.

The Middle East

During this fifth week, our prayers will be focused on the peoples, churches and countries of the Middle East.

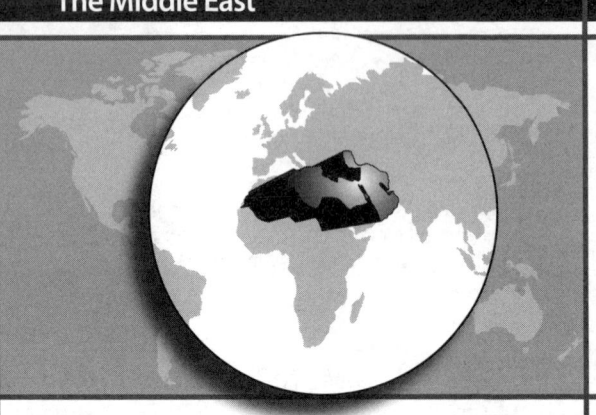

SEEK GOD

...for Christ to bless the nations with peace

Day 33
SUNDAY
MARCH 17

In your seed all the nations of the earth shall be blessed, because you have obeyed My voice. — Genesis 22:18

From the very beginning You disclosed Your purpose to Abraham, assuring Him that You intended a marvelous destiny for every people group. When Your ancient purpose comes to be fulfilled there will be tangible blessing in every language and lineage of humankind. Your blessing means that the story of every people will culminate with exhibitions of the righteousness, peace and joy of Your kingdom. We ask You to bring forth the most basic blessing: Your peace, well-being and hope upon every segment of our city. Increase this peace so that there is respect, honor and blessing flowing between the diverse peoples of our community.

Your father Abraham rejoiced to see My day, and he saw it and was glad. — John 8:56

The day of Christ, envisioned by Abraham so long ago, is the time when Christ will be glorified throughout all peoples, cultures and nations. Align the ideals and dreams of every people, so that they too will envision the peace of Christ's kingdom in their midst. Cause Your people to rejoice in confident gladness that Your peace will ultimately prevail. *Pray:*

- For trust to be restored between the diverse peoples that live in your community.
- For culturally relevant churches to be planted among every ethnicity of your city.
- For the peace of Christ to bring reconciliation in the midst of racial tension.

Seek God on behalf of **The Military**

For the gospel to spread through the special relationships of military life; for courage and protection in the danger of battle; for wisdom and the fear of the Lord when military personnel are called upon to do the work of governing and enforcing law; for grace upon chaplains and other spiritual leaders; that God will fortify families stretched by numerous moves and separations.

Prayerwalk: Pray near a military base or establishment.

A centurion came to Him, asking for help...When Jesus heard this, He was astonished and said... "I tell you the truth, I have not found anyone in Israel with such great faith."
— Matthew 8:5, 10 (NIV)

Seek God on behalf of **The Middle East**

Algeria, Bahrain, Cyprus

Day 34

**MONDAY
MARCH 18**

SEEK GOD
...for Christ to restore relationships

I have hidden My face from this city because of all their wickedness: Behold, I will bring to it health and healing, and I will heal them; and I will reveal to them an abundance of peace... It will be to Me a name of joy, praise and glory before all the nations of the earth which will hear of all the good that I do for them. – Jeremiah 33:5-6, 9

Without Your help we cannot quench the hatreds that smolder in many hearts. Verbal violence rages in many homes. Estranged children despise their parents. Minor offenses cause friendships to fail. And blood stains our streets. We'll never turn toward each other if Your face is turned away from us. Forgive our wickedness. Turn toward us in reconciling power. Bring the times of healing that You promised long ago. Sweep through our city, healing families, ending feuds and renewing the joy of friendship.

If you had known in this day, even you, the things which make for peace! But now they have been hidden from your eyes. – Luke 19:42

We have proven ourselves powerless to do more than negotiate temporary truces in the hostilities of our city. Only You, Lord Jesus, can change the hearts of people to bring forth heaven's peace. We are blind to what You bring, a grace that renews relationships of every kind. Lift the blinders from our eyes. Reveal Your ways and help us walk in them. *Pray:*

- For hostile relationships to be reconciled in Christ.
- For believers to recognize God-given opportunities to make peace in their neighborhoods and networks.

Seek God on behalf of **Broken Families**

Pray for healing of broken or embittered relationships; for comfort when a family member has passed away. Pray that the Father heart of God will overshadow children, that they would know the joy of being part of God's family; that God will meet financial needs, bring supportive friends and grant hope to many who come to follow Christ.

Prayerwalk: Apartment buildings often house fragmented families. Pray around an apartment complex, focusing prayers on those who have been bereaved or divorced.

The LORD...supports the fatherless and the widow.
– Psalm 146:9

Seek God on behalf of **The Middle East**

Egypt, Iran, Iraq

SEEK GOD
...for God to restore children to their parents

Day 35
TUESDAY
MARCH 19

All your sons will be taught of the LORD; and the well-being of your sons will be great.
— Isaiah 54:13

Many of our marriages have soured and shattered, leaving our children to learn a warped and broken way. Even the best parents have in some ways failed their children. Some have antagonized their sons and daughters, while some children have rebelled with no apparent cause. So we turn to You, our Father in heaven. Be the teacher of our homes. Heal our fractured hearts. Reconcile our children to their parents. And may Your peace be great in homes throughout our city.

And they were bringing children to Him so that He might touch them...And He took them in His arms and began blessing them, laying His hands on them.
— Mark 10:13, 16

Jesus, what kind of blessing did You pray when parents brought their kids to You? What good things did You bestow upon them? What kind of hope was in Your heart for them? In prayer, we bring our children to You now. Some of them are no longer young, but still we bring them all to You. We can imagine You taking them in Your arms, healing their hearts and touching their inmost brokenness. Give us ways to speak Your words of blessing that they would fulfill Your highest desires. *Pray:*

- For parents to be empowered to bless their children, speaking openly about God's plans for good in their lives.
- For daughters to live with single-minded zeal to love and serve Jesus.
- For sons to focus the passions of their hearts on Christ and His kingdom.

Seek God on behalf of **Laborers**

Pray that God will reveal the dignity and honor of doing work as unto Christ; that workplaces would be a setting of safety, joy and friendship; for workers to be treated with justice and dignity; for continued employment in the changing global economy; for many to follow Christ and serve Him openly in the workplace with co-laborers.

Prayerwalk: Almost every community has factories, construction sites or other places of industry. Pray for the laborers in these places.

Blessed are all who fear the LORD, who walk in His ways. You will eat the fruit of your labor; blessings and prosperity will be yours.
— Psalm 128:1-2 (NIV)

Seek God on behalf of **The Middle East**
Israel, Jordan, Kuwait

Day 36

**WEDNESDAY
MARCH 20**

SEEK GOD
...for enemies to be blessed

When a man's ways are pleasing to the LORD, he makes even his enemies to be at peace with him.
— Proverbs 16:7

We like to think of ourselves as having no personal enemies. But in fact we avoid the ones we fear and forget the ones we have wronged. We have often failed at making peace. Left to ourselves, we will only succeed in defending ourselves. We want to please You in all of our relationships. Do more than just forgive us; empower us to forgive. Train us in Your ways. Reform our attitudes. Give us hearts to bless the ones who may have harmed us. Grant us favor, even with those hostile to us, and cause us to live in peacemaking ways that please You.

But I say to you, love your enemies and pray for those who persecute you, so that you may be sons of your Father who is in heaven.
— Matthew 5:44-45

Even as Your enemies nailed You to a cross, You cried out for God to forgive them. When enemies of the cross rise up in these days with alarming strength, make us to be sons and daughters of God who endure the hostility of those who oppose You with prayers of blessing. We lift our enemies to You. Give them what none of us deserve: the forgiveness and blessing of Your love. *Pray:*

- For those hindering God's purposes to have their lives transformed by His mercy.
- That believers would love and pray for their enemies.
- For Christians suffering under oppressive governments to remain faithful, following Christ's example in all things.

Seek God on behalf of **The Athletic Industry**

Pray for those in support roles and those with higher profiles, that they will know Christ and fulfill God's calling in their lives. Pray that athletes would be good examples of dedication, commitment and courage; that they will live with integrity and carry out the responsibility of wealth and reputation; that God will reveal His calling and purpose for the students and coaches in college and university programs.

Prayerwalk: Pray on-site at the scene of an upcoming sports event near you.

Yours, O LORD, is the greatness and the power and the glory...Wealth and honor come from You... In Your hands are strength and power to exalt and give strength to all.
— 1 Chronicles 29:11-12 (NIV)

Seek God on behalf of **The Middle East**

Lebanon, Libya, Morocco

SEEK GOD
...to calm the storm of war

Day 37
THURSDAY
MARCH 21

He will judge between the nations, and will render decisions for many peoples; and they will hammer their swords into plowshares and their spears into pruning hooks. Nation will not lift up sword against nation, and never again will they learn war. – Isaiah 2:4

Calm the storm of war among the nations. Intervene by Your authority in the affairs of the nations. Accomplish what thousands of diplomats could never achieve. Isaiah's promise speaks of what You will do at the very end of the age. But we dare to ask that in our day You will move to bring an outbreak of peace that will signify, in a momentous way, the peace of the age to come. As You bring an end to relatively small conflicts in our city, reveal Yourself as the powerful peacemaking King that You are.

In His name the nations will put their hope. – Matthew 12:21 (NIV)

People from many nations have gathered in our city. Some arrived with dreams of prosperity and peace. Because some have come as captives or as refugees, there is lingering anger and despair. Despite the good intentions of nice neighbors and high-placed leaders, there has been much to disappoint nearly everyone. Now is Your time, Lord Jesus. You are the sole hope of the nations. Reveal Yourself so clearly that families, clans and entire peoples are moved to hope in You by the power of the Holy Spirit. *Pray:*

- For God to bring an end to racial or ethnic conflicts that may be present in your city.
- That the Holy Spirit will touch the nations represented in your city to recognize the unique hope of life in Jesus.

Seek God on behalf of **Ethnic Communities**

That God will bring racial harmony; that long-standing offenses may be healed by the forgiveness that begins in Jesus; that Christians show honor and act in Christ's reconciling power; that the beauty of distinctive languages and cultures would be on display in local churches.

Prayerwalk: Pray blessings in a neighborhood with an ethnic identity different than your own; or pray blessings upon a business owned by people of another ethnicity than yours.

All the ends of the earth will remember and turn to the LORD, and all the families of the nations will bow down before him.
– Psalm 22:27 (NIV)

Seek God on behalf of **The Middle East**
Oman, Qatar, Saudi Arabia

Day 38
FRIDAY MARCH 22

SEEK GOD
...to gather all peoples in worship

This will be written for the generation to come, that a people yet to be created may praise the LORD...When the peoples are gathered together, and the kingdoms, to serve the LORD. – Psalm 102:18, 22

What has been promised must be fulfilled: that You will save and gather a people from all peoples. Since the day Christ rose from the dead You have been forming this new people. This global people will name You with praise that resonates throughout the earth. We long to hear that song. But at this hour we are not yet gathered as one people. We still find ourselves separated and segregated in our cities. Hear us as we unite our prayers. Look with favor upon us as we gather to serve You in worship. Assemble us before You as one family drawn together from many peoples.

He began to teach and say to them, "Is it not written: 'My house will be called a house of prayer for all nations.'" – Mark 11:17

Keep on teaching us so that we blaze with bright hope for the destiny of all peoples. The global people You are forming will become so diverse and numerous that we will never fit in our church buildings. Be pleased with our humble gatherings, but form us to be a house made without hands, with people summoned from every culture, language and race. Call diverse assemblies of the nations that You have brought to our city. Cause us to worship You together in the Spirit and in truth. Gather us and make Your home with us.
Pray:

- For city-wide worship events that will bring the community together in festive praise.
- For divided denominations and traditions to find unity in worshiping Jesus Christ.

Seek God on behalf of **The Unborn**

That these precious children will be acknowledged and honored by all; for each of them to find sheltering homes; that the awful waste of their lives would cease; that they would come to Christ at an early age; for the parents of unborn babies, that God would turn their hearts toward their children.

Prayerwalk: As you pray for your neighbors or coworkers, pray that God will break the power of self-centered lifestyles that disregard children, and that He will forgive and heal those who have harmed their children in any way.

For He will deliver...the afflicted who have no one to help. He will...save the need from death. He will rescue them from oppression and violence, for precious is the blood in His sight.
– Psalm 72:12-14 (NIV)

Seek God on behalf of **The Middle East**
Syria, Tunisia, Turkey

SEEK GOD

...for Christ's Lordship to be welcomed by the nations

Day 39
SATURDAY
MARCH 23

Rejoice greatly, O daughter of Zion! Shout in triumph, O daughter of Jerusalem! Behold, your king is coming to you. He is just and endowed with salvation, humble, and mounted on a donkey...And the bow of war will be cut off. And He will speak peace to the nations; and His dominion will be from sea to sea.
— Zechariah 9:9-10

Before You come to bring an end to the age, You will come in triumphant humility, bringing Your salvation. Somehow Your voice will be lifted up, speaking so that everyone will hear. Your voice will be gentle, disarming evil powers without conventional weapons. Already many have heard Your voice. Already You have been speaking peace in the midst of war. We welcome You as You come to our community. Without waging a war of conquest, You have already conquered our hearts. You will soon be utterly victorious over evil. Come magnificent King! Our hope is fixed on You.

And as Jesus returned, the people welcomed Him, for they had all been waiting for Him. — Luke 8:40

We cannot know when You will come again, but find us watching when You do. Some of us burn with passionate yearning for Your return. Others are indifferent or even fearful. Capture the hearts of all who name You as Lord. Increase our hope so that we love Your kingdom and Your appearing. Even so, come, Lord Jesus. *Pray:*

- That Jesus will be expected and loved by many who will wait eagerly for His return.
- For Christians to prepare their city for Christ's coming by their prayer, evangelism and service.
- For a visitation of Christ's peace-bringing presence to be welcomed by millions across the face of the earth.

Seek God on behalf of **Elderly People**

That God's strength and peace will be poured out on everyone who is advanced in years. Pray that they may be honored, that they may be cared for; that loneliness be banished through lasting friendships and family bonds; that sickness be lifted; that they may live to see their prayers answered; that their latter years will be significant, reflecting the glory of God.

Prayerwalk: Pray for the oldest person you know in your neighborhood. Or pray at a retirement community or an extended care facility.

Now Abraham was old, advanced in age; and the LORD had blessed Abraham in every way.
— Genesis 24:1

Seek God on behalf of **The Middle East**

United Arab Emirates, Yemen

Seeking His **Visitation**
Welcoming Christ our King

The event we have come to call "Palm Sunday" shines as a prophetic portrait of the spiritual awakening Christ desires to bring.

Imparting a vision of His visitation

Jesus initiated the procession and refused to shut it down. He was doing more than merely fulfilling prophecy. He was prophesying, presenting a lasting vision of how He will be recognized in the midst of hostility at the end of the age. Christ will be followed by some from every people. He will be welcomed, at least by a few, in every place. Palm Sunday gives us a way to pray toward a global spiritual awakening.

Preparing the way by prayer

Jesus prepared the way for Palm Sunday by sending His followers to pray on-site in many communities (Luke 10:1-2). The prayers of these ordinary followers were publicly prayed and then openly answered. God was being honored. Jesus was becoming famous in places where He had not personally visited.

A crescendo of welcoming praise

The raising of Lazarus touched off an explosion of welcoming praise (John 12:18). The dramatic answer to Jesus' prayer for His friend Lazarus (John 11:41-43) got everyone talking about all they had seen God do in the lives of their friends and neighbors. Luke says the crowd was praising God "for all the miracles which they had seen" (Luke 19:37). Grateful praise for many answered prayers quickly became a crescendo of welcoming worship.

Palm Sunday: The hope of Christ's visitation

A lasting movement

Thousands of people gathered at the temple with Jesus early every morning, hanging on every word He said (Luke 21:38). The Palm Sunday worshipers should not be confused with the much smaller mob that shouted for Jesus' execution later that week. That crowd was incited by Christ's enemies, who were forced to arrest Jesus by night "because they were afraid of the people"—the very throng that had welcomed and worshiped Him daily with increasing devotion (Luke 22:2, Mark 14:1-2).

A prophetic portrait

Palm Sunday is sometimes dismissed as if it was a political rally gone wrong. But Jesus was for it. He planned whatever could have been planned. And He refused to silence the celebration. He said that rocks would have cried out if the people had been restrained (Luke 19:40). The intensity mounted. The crowds increased. Eventually "all the city was stirred, saying, 'Who is this?'" (Matthew 21:10). Those who hadn't yet encountered Jesus were eager to know more. If Jesus was giving us any indication of how God desires to visit communities with transforming power, we have grounds to pray for such receptive glory to sweep throughout whole cities in our day.

Our best hope—Our only hope

Hated or praised, Christ was then what He will be again: the sole focus of attention of whole cities in days of great spiritual awakening. Our best prayers are prayers of welcome—that the risen Jesus Himself will be recognized and received throughout entire communities.

More about His arrival than our revival

Now, more than ever, it's time to invite Christ the Lord to bring His life-giving presence upon our cities.

> Whenever there has been revival, it has been a partial fulfillment of the promise of Palm Sunday.

Day 40

PALM SUNDAY
MARCH 24

SEEK GOD
...for Christ to visit our communities

On the first Palm Sunday, the crowds shouted phrases from Psalm 118, which was one of the songs traditionally sung at the Passover holiday. Our prayers on this Palm Sunday spring from those very words.

The stone the builders rejected
has become the capstone. — Psalm 118:22

Jesus—the one who had been rejected, denied and overlooked—was put on display on Palm Sunday. He was exalted in the view of some, and yet dismissed by others. Some remained determined to reject Him, but no one ignored Him.

And so we pray for our community. Bring a day when every eye beholds Him, even those who have opposed or overlooked Him.

The LORD has done this,
and it is marvelous in our eyes.
This is the day the LORD has made.
Let us rejoice and be glad in it.
— Psalm 118:23-24

Suddenly it became clear that the Almighty God was visiting with transforming power. To many it seemed that heaven was near enough to touch.

Open our eyes to recognize what You are doing to glorify Your Son. Give Your people joy in welcoming the long-expected surprise of Christ's visitation.

O LORD, save us! [literally: Hosanna]
O LORD, push things forward to finish.
Blessed is He who comes
in the name of the LORD.'"
— Psalm 118:25-26 (Translation by author)

Many suddenly saw that they could be saved in ways they hadn't ever thought possible before. They could see You rushing Your purpose to Your intended goal, so that the glories of Your character would flourish in communities everywhere.

Open our eyes to see Jesus coming to our city. Arouse a hope in us that He will save us more than we've ever been saved. We say, "Yes!" to Him. We welcome Him now with joy. He has come, but He will yet come to reveal the name and glory of God.

The LORD is God, and
He has given us light. — Psalm 118:27

Palm Sunday stands as a fact behind us, but it also looms large and beautiful before us as a promise of Christ's visitation.

Lord God, give us light to welcome Jesus. Make Him marvelous in our eyes. Make us steady in hope and eager in expectancy. Give light to many throughout our city, that Jesus will be welcomed, followed and loved.

...with His presence and transforming power

*When He came near...the whole crowd of disciples
began joyfully to praise God in loud voices
for all the miracles they had seen:
"Blessed is the king who comes
in the name of the Lord!
Peace in heaven and glory in the highest!"
Some of the Pharisees in the crowd said to Jesus,
"Teacher, rebuke Your disciples!"
"I tell you," He replied, "if they keep quiet,
the stones will cry out."*
— Luke 19:37-40 (NIV)

As we celebrate the remembrance of Your coming to the city of Jerusalem, our hearts surge forward in hope that You will soon visit our city–and many others–to bring about a great awakening to Your Lordship.

May the rocks keep silent before the escalating sound of welcoming worship. May our children be the first to know and honor You. May millions submit their lives to You and be saved. Let the peace be as great as Your glory.

Even so, come, Lord Jesus.

Seek God on behalf of
The Coming Generation

How often I wanted to gather your children together, the way a hen gathers her chicks under her wings, and you were unwilling...You will not see Me until you say, "Blessed is He who comes in the name of the Lord."
— Matthew 23:37, 39

That many who are now small children would soon become passionate followers of Christ; that during their lifetimes they will finish evangelizing the world; that they will endure suffering to overcome evil and bring forth the promised blessing of God upon all peoples; that they will give Christ the finest whole-life worship of all history.

Prayerwalk: Walk your city thinking of the people who will live there in years to come, should the Lord delay His second coming. Pray for the generation that will be dwelling in your city when Christ returns.

Seek God on behalf of
Jerusalem

Pray for God's peace and glory to be upon Jerusalem.

PRAYERCONNECT

Connecting to the heart of Christ through prayer

A new bimonthly magazine designed to:

Equip prayer leaders and pastors with tools to disciple their congregations.

Connect intercessors with the growing worldwide prayer movement.

Mobilize believers to pray God's purposes for their church, city and the nations.

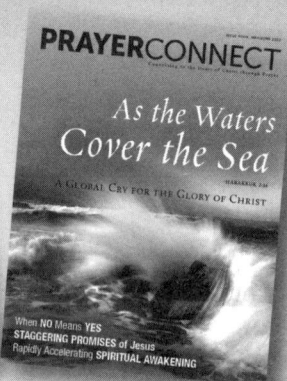

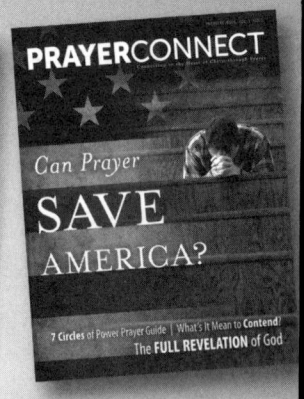

Each issue of **PRAYER**CONNECT includes 48 pages of:

- Practical articles to equip and inspire your prayer life.
- Helpful prayer tips and proven ideas.
- News of prayer movements around the world.
- Theme articles exploring important prayer topics.
- Connections to prayer resources available online.

Three different ways to subscribe *(six issues a year)*:

$24.99 - **Print** *(includes digital version)*
$19.99 - **Digital**
$30.00 - **Membership** in Church Prayer Leaders Network *(includes print, digital and CPLN benefits)*

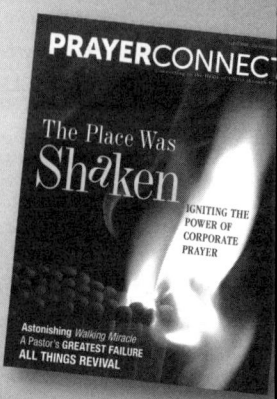

Subscribe now.
Order at www.prayerconnect.net or call 800-217-5200.

PRAYERCONNECT *is sponsored by: America's National Prayer Committee, Denominational Prayer Leaders Network and The International Prayer Council.*

FreshPrayer

Pray from ancient truths for urgent needs

FreshPrayer is a free, single-page prayer guide, available on the WayMakers website (www.waymakers.org). Each issue is designed to help you find clear, relevant ways to pray from specific scriptures for particular needs and concerns of people who are far from Christ.

Scripture-rich authority. Life-giving clarity. Everyday simplicity. It's perfect for small groups looking for innovative ways to pray together for people who don't yet know Christ.

Ideas for those who facilitate gatherings. Every issue consists of two items: a single-page participant's guide to be copied for everyone in your group; and a single-page leader's guide that provides ideas to guide lively prayer sessions. The pdf files can be downloaded from the WayMakers website. Five issues are currently available. A new issue will be released every two months (sometimes more often). It's an ideal way to continue to pray beyond *Seek God for the City*.

Guided, grounded and focused. The most engaging prayer gatherings are usually *guided* by a facilitator who invites participants to form simple and sincere requests that are *grounded* in the truths of the Bible and *focused* on specific issues in the lives of others.

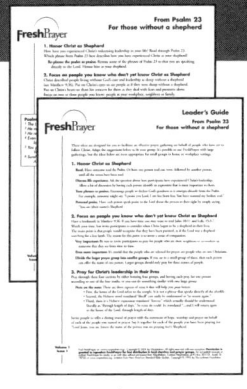

Each issue contains a leader's guide and a participant's guide. Download FreshPrayer at no cost at waymakers.org.

Put a copy in the hands of everyone who gathers to pray. Selected verses are laid out alongside creative ideas that help people unite and focus intercessory prayer for those without Christ.

Praying with faith, hope and love for our Muslim neighbors

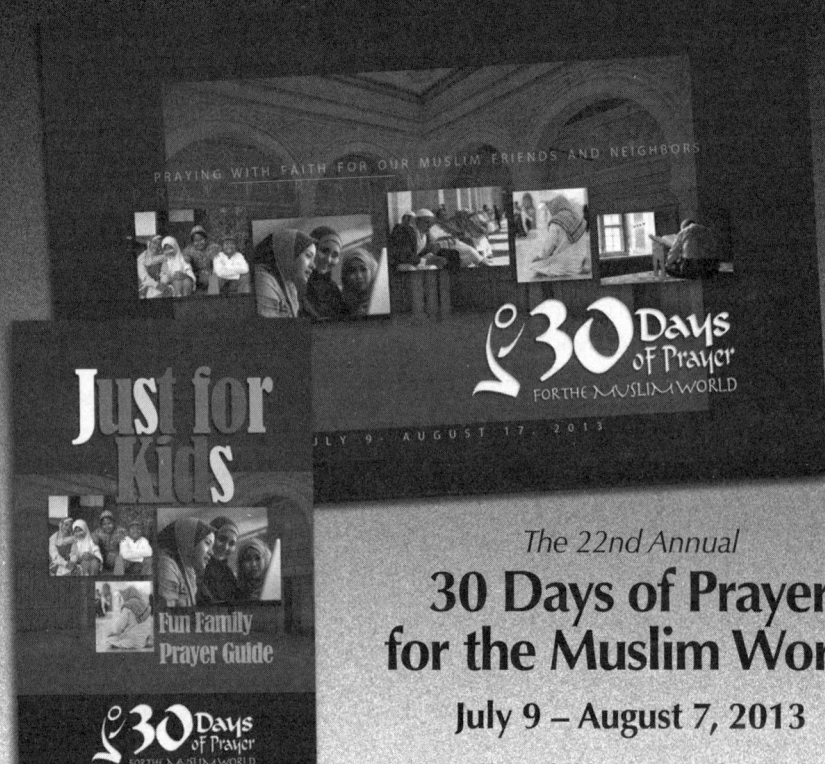

The 22nd Annual
30 Days of Prayer for the Muslim World
July 9 – August 7, 2013

Join millions of Christians around the world who participate each year in this largest ongoing international prayer focus on the Muslim world.

Coinciding with Ramadan, Christians worldwide are called to make an intentional effort to learn about, pray for and reach out to Muslim neighbors—across the street and around the world

Media sound bites about Islamic extremism can too easily incite anger, fear and even hatred toward Muslims. Instead, pray with the mind and heart of Christ. This full-color prayer guide—available in both adult and kids versions—is a proven tool helping Christians to understand and to persistent pray for Muslim neighbors and nations.

To find out more, or to order go to:
www.30DaysPrayer.com

Or email:
paulf@30DaysPrayer.com

Or write:
**WorldChristian.com "30 Days"
PO Box 9208
Colorado Springs, CO 80932**

WORLDCHRISTIAN.COM
Resources and Ministry that Impact Our World

30 Days of Prayer
PRAYING FOR OUR WORLD

Pray with the world.

THE GLOBAL Day of Prayer

**Pentecost Sunday
May 19, 2013**

Focus prayer with the Ten-Day Prayer Guide, available in pdf format on-line. Unite the prayers of your congregation with churches across the globe on Pentecost Sunday using the "Prayer for the World."

- One day of prayer on Pentecost Sunday, May 19, 2013.
- Ten days of continuous prayer, May 9 - 18, 2013.
- Ninety days of blessing, May 20 - August 17, 2013.

Since the dawn of this century, Christians all over the world have gathered on Pentecost Sunday for a day of repentance and prayer. Many gatherings have been large-scale public events. Even more have been small gatherings in churches and homes. Find all you need on the website: a downloadable Ten-Day Prayer Guide, resources to help congregations pray the "Prayer for the World" on Pentecost and an all-new guide for the ninety days of blessing.

For info and prayer guides go to
www.gdopusa.com or
www.globaldayofprayer.com

GLOBAL DAY OF PRAYER

WayMakers Resources

ITEM	DISCOUNT	COST *	QUANTITY	TOTAL
SEEK GOD FOR THE CITY 2013				
or CLAMA A DIOS POR LA CIUDAD 2013 **				
1-19 copies		$ 3.00 each		
20-99 copies	20%	$ 2.40 each		
100-249 copies	35%	$ 1.95 each		
250-499 copies	55%	$ 1.35 each		
PROMPTS FOR PRAYERWALKERS		$ 2.00 each		
LIGHT FROM MY HOUSE		$ 2.00 each		
OPEN MY CITY		$ 2.00 each		
WHAT WOULD JESUS PRAY?		$ 2.00 each		
BLESSINGS		$ 2.00 each		
THE LORD IS THEIR SHEPHERD		$ 2.00 each		
PRAYERWALKING	25%	$ 9.00 each		

SHIPPING & HANDLING

Subtotal	S & H Total
$ 1 – $ 10	$ 5.00
$ 11 – $ 30	$ 7.00
$ 31 – $ 75	20% of order
$ 76 – $ 115	15% of order
$ 116 and up	12% of order

Subtotal
Texas residents add 8.25% sales tax
Shipping and Handling (Minimum $ 5)
Donation to WayMakers (Optional)
TOTAL

PLEASE SHIP TO: *(Please provide a street address. UPS cannot deliver to a Post Office Box.)*

Name

Organization

Street Address

City   State   ZIP

Phone   E-mail

VISA / MC / Discover   Expires

Name on card

* Please call to learn about quantity discounts (up to 60%) on most items!

** *Seek God for the City* in Spanish is available at the same prices. Order online, or call us to combine English and Spanish in the same order. *Clama a Dios por la Ciudad* está disponible al mismo precio que en inglés. Llámenos para combinar libros en inglés y español en la misma orden.

Please order early to allow normal delivery time of two weeks (but many orders can be fulfilled last minute!) Additional shipping may be required after February 1. Supplies are limited. Order before January 25 to be sure of getting all the copies you need. Please include payment with your order. Please calculate and include payment for shipping costs. Thanks! For quickest delivery, call us. Make checks payable to WayMakers. Please send this form with payment to:

WayMakers
PO Box 203131
Austin, TX 78720-3131

Phone   (512) 419-7729
            (800) 264-5214
Fax   (512) 323-9066
Web   www.waymakers.org